Escape to
Clayoquot
Sound

T0265601

Finding Home in a Wild Place

Escape to Clayoquot Sound

JOHN DOWD

AND BEA DOWD

Copyright © 2024 John Dowd and Bea Dowd

Excerpt on page 143 from *Cougar Annie's Garden* by Margaret Horsfield (1999). Used by permission of Margaret Horsfield.

All rights reserved. No part of this publication may be reproduced, stored in a retrieval system, or transmitted in any form or by any means—electronic, mechanical, audio recording, or otherwise—without the written permission of the publisher or a licence from Access Copyright, Toronto, Canada.

Heritage House Publishing Company Ltd.
heritagehouse.ca

Cataloguing information available from Library and Archives Canada
978-1-77203-471-4 (paperback)
978-1-77203-472-1 (e-book)

Edited by Andrea Lister
Cover and interior book design by Setareh Ashrafologhalai
Cover and interior photographs by John and Bea Dowd unless otherwise indicated
Maps by Eric Leinberger

The interior of this book was produced on FSC®-certified, acid-free paper, processed chlorine free, and printed with vegetable-based inks.

The authors gratefully acknowledge that Vargas Island, the setting for their nine years on the outer coast, is part of the unceded traditional territories of the ʕaaḥuusʔatḥ (Ahousaht) and qiłcmaʔatḥ (Keltsmaht) Peoples, who together form the ʕaaḥuusʔatḥ (Ahousaht) First Nation of Maaqtusiis (Marktosis).

Heritage House gratefully acknowledges that the land on which we live and work is within the traditional territories of the Lkwungen (Esquimalt and Songhees), Malahat, Pacheedaht, Scia'new, T'Sou-ke, and W̱SÁNEĆ (Pauquachin, Tsartlip, Tsawout, Tseycum) Peoples.

We acknowledge the financial support of the Government of Canada through the Canada Book Fund (CBF) and the Canada Council for the Arts, and the Province of British Columbia through the British Columbia Arts Council and the Book Publishing Tax Credit.

28 27 26 25 24   1 2 3 4 5

Printed in China

To each other

CONTENTS

Northern abalone,
now endangered.

FOREWORD
AH YES, I REMEMBER IT WELL...

A HOUSE IS a shell we make or we find: we found ours and, like hermit crabs, made it home, this for nearly a decade. These were our best years, because of the beauty we saw and the adventures we lived; because age gave us the perspective to know what mattered and what did not.

We live in the shell no longer, but it lives in us. Enough so that we want to share what we know now about that certain beach house on Vargas Island. A simple house, pinned, sun-bleached, and wind-battered, at the edge and at the heart of Clayoquot Sound.

It will have changed a great deal by now—houses do that. But in our minds, it stays what it was then: perfect in its imperfections, beautiful, quirky, a window and a gateway to an ever-changing natural realm.

For this chronicle, no journals were kept. The text is knitted from the scant correspondence we kept, the photos we took, and our joint, imperfect, and often hilariously mismatched recollections. The events are real, the timing could be suspect. Though we definitely took turns at being wrong, it was, John felt, a bit like the song from that old film musical, *Gigi*, where Maurice Chevalier marvels at how well he remembers, and Hermione Gingold sets him straight at every turn. To wit, the Clayoquot version:

JOHN: We came in June

BEA: The month was May

HE: We stayed a week

SHE: Only a day.

HE: Of course ... I remember it now.
We ate fresh fish

SHE: No, bread and cheese

HE: Then hiked the beach

SHE: We cut some trees.

HE: Ah yes, I remember so well.
A Northerly blew

SHE: It was calm that day
With a hint of rain.

HE: That's true
I remember it too.

A joint effort.

Most of the text is in John's voice, with me now and again weaving in my own gleanings and recollections in a distinct typeface, more so beyond year one. I handled fact-checking and research but mostly we worked together on the project, mixing it up as needed. We went as low as poaching each other's stories. A duet, if at times a duel.

BEA DOWD

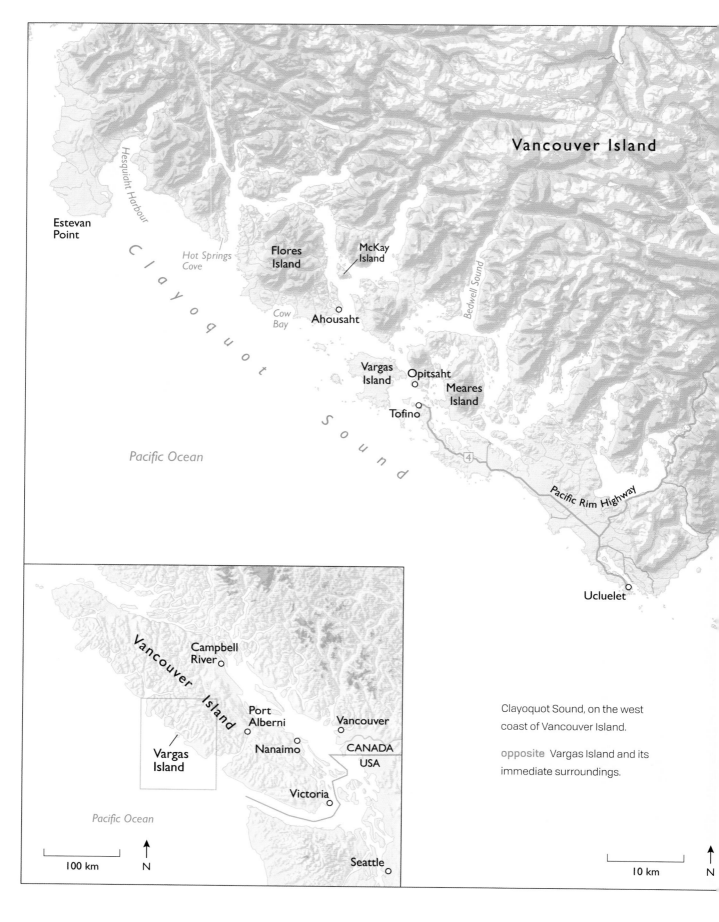

Vancouver Island

Estevan
Point

Hesquiaht Harbour

Clayoquot Sound

Hot Springs
Cove

Flores
Island

McKay
Island

Bedwell Sound

Cow
Bay

Ahousaht

Vargas
Island

Opitsaht

Meares
Island

Tofino

Pacific Ocean

4

Pacific Rim Highway

Ucluelet

Vancouver Island

Campbell
River

Port
Alberni

Vancouver

CANADA
USA

Nanaimo

Vargas
Island

Victoria

Pacific Ocean

Seattle

100 km   N

Clayoquot Sound, on the west
coast of Vancouver Island.

opposite Vargas Island and its
immediate surroundings.

10 km   N

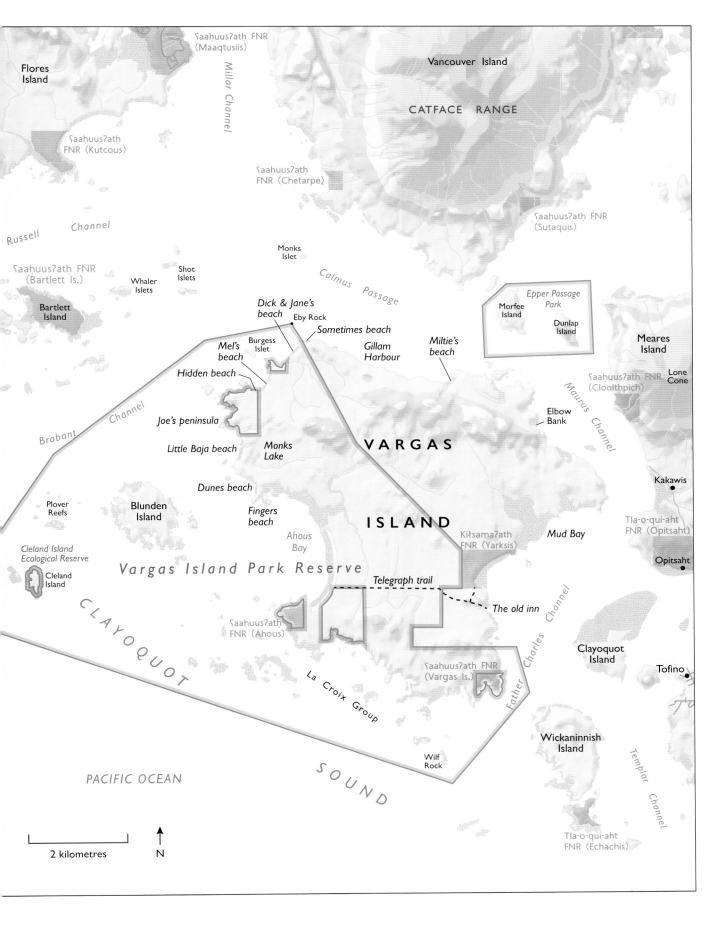

Flores
Island

ʕaahuusʔath FNR
(Maaqtusiis)

Vancouver Island

CATFACE RANGE

ʕaahuusʔath
FNR (Kutcous)

ʕaahuusʔath
FNR (Chetarpe)

ʕaahuusʔath FNR
(Sutaquis)

Russell   Channel

ʕaahuusʔath FNR
(Bartlett Is.)

Shot
Islets

Whaler
Islets

Monks
Islet

Calmus   Passage

Epper Passage
Park

Morfee
Island

Dunlap
Island

Meares
Island

Bartlett
Island

Dick & Jane's
beach

Eby Rock

Sometimes beach

Gillam
Harbour

Miltie's
beach

Lone
Cone

ʕaahuusʔath FNR
(Cloolthpich)

Burgess
Islet

Mel's
beach

Hidden beach

Brabant   Channel

Joe's peninsula

Little Baja beach

Monks
Lake

VARGAS

Elbow
Bank

Maurus   Channel

Dunes beach

Blunden
Island

Plover
Reefs

Fingers
beach

Ahous
Bay

ISLAND

Kiɬsamaʔath
FNR (Yarksis)

Mud Bay

Kakawis

Tla-o-qui-aht
FNR (Opitsaht)

Opitsaht

Cleland Island
Ecological Reserve

Cleland
Island

Vargas   Island   Park   Reserve

Telegraph trail

The old inn

ʕaahuusʔath
FNR (Ahous)

CLAYOQUOT

Clayoquot
Island

Tofino

Father   Charles   Channel

La Croix Group

ʕaahuusʔath FNR
(Vargas Is.)

Wickaninnish
Island

SOUND

Wilf
Rock

Templar   Channel

PACIFIC OCEAN

Tla-o-qui-aht
FNR (Echachis)

2 kilometres

N

South Rocks, low
cloud rolling in.

INTRODUCTION
TRESPASS

SPRING 2004. VIEWED FROM the beach, the buildings blended nicely into the surrounding forest. There were two of them. The house, tucked in behind a broken snag, had a large bay window and a porch down one side. Facing it was a workshop from which the windows had been removed. Sheathed in sun-bleached shakes, they sat atop a six-metre bank beyond a fringe of glossy green salal bushes. A corduroy ramp led to a grassy patch between the two. At the bottom of the ramp sat a sturdy boathouse built on skids, tied with a ship's hawser to a bent hemlock that curved out from the bank.

Untrampled grass grew up to broad steps that led to the covered porch. Overhead joints had been carefully notched and spiked, and the front door looked unusually thick, inset with a tall oval window. A couple of straight-backed chairs sat beside a round of cedar that served as a table; on it, an enamel cup held the desiccated remains of coffee and bugs. From this vantage point, one would be able to watch the sun set over the Shot Islets.

At the back of the house, tall south-facing windows looked onto an ancient cedar that branched into a mossy, fern-encrusted candelabra. Nearby was another cedar, tall, silvery, and dead, its branches reaching skyward as if in a final appeal to the heavens.

To the north, the panoramic window I'd seen from the beach offered a view of the verdant slopes of Flores Island and the low, forested peninsula that obscured Ahousaht on the Marktosis Reserve.

I pressed on the front door. It resisted momentarily, then yielded. Against my better instincts, I went in.

It was like entering an old sailing ship. Driftwood logs had been notched into a sparse post-and-beam frame with naturally bent braces, every feature built-in: two upholstered bunk-style couches, nooks of fitted shelves, and, beneath the paned windows with their display of old bottles, looking out over the beach, a wide, chest-high workbench surfaced with wooden tiles. The floor was of coarse planks worn smooth. Thick spiral steps built of golden hardwood and notched into a heavily weathered driftwood post gave access to a loft. There, a home-built double bed surrounded by empty bookshelves and an empty closet occupied most of the space. Clearly, whoever had lived here was no longer in residence and, judging from the dust, had left some time ago. At the far end of the sleeping gallery, a narrow, solid door by a diamond-shaped window opened onto a wide, skylit mezzanine above the south-facing room. It looked a bit rough. Tar-papered back wall, half the space a jumble of old cardboard boxes and newspapers. In all other respects, the perfect studio space.

I proceeded back to the living room to find a small kitchen two steps down. On one side, it had a stainless-steel sink and old-fashioned water pump, with a corner cupboard by a window that looked into a thicket of young alder. On the other, another wood tile bench resting on twin cupboards and flanked with enclosed shelves. A porch-side window stuck with a blue Audubon decal offered a view of the corduroy ramp. The latches on the cupboard doors had been carefully carved of the same golden hardwood as the stairs. Every shake was carefully cut to fit its companion. All edges of the shakes had been scalloped with a very sharp tool.

The cupboards were empty except for one that held a first aid kit and some ancient cans of pop, gritty on top from being washed ashore. Against the north wall, a small, rusty old box-type wood stove was attached to an equally rusty chimney running through the ceiling and the loft. The floor was made from short, end-grain rounds of cedar, the gaps filled with old cement.

A thick door led to the sunroom seen from the mezzanine: almost six metres high and crisscrossed with driftwood beams and braces. Light came from two huge, slightly clouded vertical panes meeting at an outward angle at the back, West Coast style, and two wide side windows. There was also a pair of Plexiglas

Behind the unlocked door, our future?

skylights. A friendly, joyful place to be, I thought; airy as a ship's deck, yet fully protected. The floor here was made of rectangular cedar blocks, set into a loose mix of sand, pebbles, and broken shells. A large square table occupied the centre space, surrounded by bins and buckets of sand, garden materials, and kindling. To one side of the kitchen doorway was a two-ring gas cooker set on a built-in cabinet; to the other, a tool bench bereft of tools, with some construction sketches drawn on tarpaper above it. Beyond the tool bench, a back door, this one lightweight with a sliding bolt lock.

Outside again, I breathed a little freer. A chilly wind swept across the beach from the north. I tried to imagine living here, surrounded by wind-scarred forest giants amid a sea of salal.

The workshop had an open doorway and consisted of one large room with nine metres of sturdy workbench backed by window gaps with a beach view on two sides. Skylights cast a yellow glow onto a low worktable in the centre. The missing windows were intact and stacked in a corner. The workshop was full of pulpy firewood casting a melancholy mood over what had clearly once been a fine workplace. Moss-encrusted lumber lay against the back wall, and a dark stain on the dirt floor drew my attention to a leak in the roof.

A rusty vintage tractor with salal sprouting through the steering mechanism occupied the open end of the building farthest from the sea. Beyond that was an outside table piled with rotting lumber, and across an expanse of salal lay a badly corroded boat trailer and the upturned relic of a wooden rowboat.

At the back of the workshop, a door led to a small generator room from which the generator had been removed, though the wiring was still in place. Offcuts of steel were scattered behind the workshop. *Mad Max* came to mind: every square yard of the spongy, mossy grounds out back was littered with flotsam, jetsam, plastic pipe, steel offcuts, and polystyrene trash.

"Well, I've found the place I want to live," I announced when I returned to the crew back at camp.

My companions looked at me in disbelief.

"You mean that old cabin at the end of the beach?" Gerry asked.

"It's perfect," I said. "Needs work; a bit gloomy, but we can change that."

A few days before, I had flown over the area for a sea kayak video project, not noticing the cabin from the air.

The Tofino Air seaplane had roared and vibrated its way along the coast from its home dock while I pressed my nose to the window, soaking in as much of the view as I could. Scattered islands and ragged coves of black rock laced with white stretched to the horizon. Dawson, our intrepid cameraman/director, poked his lens through the open window, camera winking its red running light. It was a glorious day for filming.

As Vargas Island crept closer, a more tormented coastline came into view. Ocean swells lashed the La Croix islets at the southern end, rocks awash with foam. Dawson tapped the pilot and pointed down. We dipped low till we could clearly see the faces of people aboard a small fishing boat weaving a course around a gigantic bed of bull kelp. Then on up to the sweep of bright white sand at Ahous Bay with its drab swamp hinterland.

More sandy beaches: Dunes, Little Baja, and Dick and Jane's with its sandspit that almost reached Burgess Islet.

"That's where we'll be filming the next on-water stuff," Dawson yelled.

I nodded as we turned east past Catface Mountain. Hard to see the face of a cat in that old logging scar, I thought as we floated past at eye level from it. Below were a handful of squatter cabins, tucked into various coves along Calmus Passage—then the near slopes of Meares Island, steep and heavily forested still.

Meares Island: the site of the first blockade in the decade-long War in the Woods, pitting loggers against a coalition of environmentalists, Indigenous groups, and hippies in their claims over old-growth forest starting in the mid-'80s. The fight had split the community of Tofino down the middle, a division that persisted still, judging from the bumper sticker I had recently seen of a revving chainsaw on a battered pickup: THINK FAST HIPPIE. It was a scar gradually being healed by the money tourism brought as gentrification took hold in the rough fishing and logging town.

I returned to Vancouver with pictures of the cabin to show Bea.

"It needs work and a mood change," I said. "Our nearest neighbours would be Neil and Marilyn at the Vargas Island Inn. Four hours hike to the south and across the island."

Bea already knew something of the area from our video shoots. She had been with us the night we got lost in fog in Neil's leaky skiff on our way to make a video of, of all things, navigation. She was ready for adventure. Our kids were grown, doing their own thing. We'd travelled all we wanted. And from our fifteen years in a log cabin on Hollyburn Mountain above Vancouver, we already knew a thing or two about living off-grid.

"It's owned by Mel, an American draft dodger," I said, digging a folded paper from my wallet and spreading it on the table by the phone.

We arranged to visit Mel at his Victoria home the next weekend. A sleepy-eyed, moustachioed man with a gentle smile, he took us in through the garage, where he had his work furnace. Mel was a glass artist, a serious one. He had also been a trader in antiques and memorabilia. Everything in his handsome, vintage house reflected this, including a 1952 refrigerator that he proudly opened and closed to let us hear the quiet hum. His low-lit living room would have provided the perfect film-noir background for Hitchcock and his smoke rings. The ambient smell, however, was not smoke. Mel volunteered that his wife was currently fostering five cats—which was in part why they couldn't spend much time on Vargas. Also, he said, "She doesn't love it like I do."

From our conversation, it turned out he owned not one but two (maybe even three) cabins on a four-hectare lot that took in the south end of Dick and Jane's beach as well as the peninsula across to the next beach down (Mel's beach, appropriately enough), where he had a workshop of his own.

Mel had mentioned he didn't much like kayakers when we'd first spoken, so we knew to be careful around the topic. It helped that we were no longer in the business, at least not as merchants. But what was it about kayakers? we asked. "They were a plague in the '80s and '90s," he said. "Hundreds of them taking over the beach in their carnival tents, pooping in the woods, festooning the place with toilet paper." The memory of it was enough to upset his usual soft monotone.

"So then," he asked after a lengthy pause, "why should I rent the place to you?"

"We like it, it's what we've been looking for, and we're pretty good at leaving things better than we found them," I offered as brightly as I could.

It turns out our timing was good. He was anxious to have someone living there to reduce potential pillage and we were not Tofino locals, who might have wanted to use the place mainly as a surfers' party house.

"Okay," he said. "You can have it for fifteen hundred, on condition you don't cut down any trees more than twelve inches across."

I must have frowned.

"Fifteen hundred a year," he clarified.

We left with a handwritten agreement giving us first option to buy the place because, who knew?

And Bea hadn't even been there yet.

The first coho.

1

FIRST SEASON

A WEEK LATER, Bea and I borrowed a friend's old Mazda, loaded a double kayak onto the roof, then headed to Tofino. The plan was to meet Mel for a walk through the property and get a close-up look at what we were getting into.

Although we had been in the kayak business for more than a decade, running both a shop and a magazine, Bea and I had not often paddled together during that time, or in the intervening decade and a half.[1] For her especially, what had been our way of life had lost some of its shine as it became our work.

We launched from a rocky cove near the Tofino government dock. Cobber, our border collie, stood by the boat watching while Bea secured her spray skirt. His ears and tail drooped. Resigned, he walked slowly to the water's edge.

"Come on," I said impatiently.

He licked his lips then waded out and put one paw on the coaming: he'd done his bit. I pulled his front half aboard then hoisted his rear end in by the base of his tail and pushed him down between my knees. He settled onto his foam pad and gave me one last baleful look before I secured the spray skirt above his head. We pushed off and took up our paddles.

As we picked up speed it started to feel like old times. Sea grass caressed the hull as we glided over the shallow bank to Father Charles Channel. It was the start of another adventure, and that felt good. Adventure was, after all, what our lives together had been about. It was the reason the twenty-three-year-old Québécoise took off alone to South America where we met. It was also the reason we married just three months later, then paddled a double kayak from Venezuela to Miami along the Caribbean island chain. Eighteen hundred kilometres, nine months. Our honeymoon.

To starboard, the houses of the Tla-o-qui-aht community of Opitsaht on Meares Island stretched like a string of coloured beads between forested Lone Cone Mountain and a shallow beach where a dozen half-wild cattle foraged on kelp. Ahead, waves kicked up a chop as the tide flooded north toward Bedwell Sound, a deep cut in Vancouver Island at the back of Meares. The kayak was a good, fast twenty-one-footer that could accommodate a standard cooler amidships, as well as dry storage fore and aft and room for a compliant dog inside the cockpit. We could cover the almost thirteen kilometres from Tofino to our beach in two hours, give or take.

Just short of a large building and dock marked on the chart as Kakawis, we took a direct line across the shallow Elbow Bank to the rocky north coast of Vargas, where forest spilled into the sea. Sport fishing boats and water taxis from Ahousaht sped by between us and land, following the curved shoreline channel and tossing colliding wakes our way. Then came the whale-watching boats, ten-metre rigid inflatables (RIBS) with twin 300-horsepower outboards, their red-suited tourists arranged in rows like LEGO people, hanging on for dear life as they blasted by.

Beyond Elbow Bank, we hugged the shore, ducking into coves to avoid the traffic. Here, the water was clear enough to see the gently waving kelp, shelter to schools of silver needlefish that turned sharply in unison as the kayaks ghosted them. We nipped between shore and a scattering of deep green, high-backed button islands.

Three kayaks lay on the sand at Miltie's beach. Smoke from a campfire drifted across the water. From here the view was of Catface and beyond it the steep hills of Flores. The current, which floods both ways around Vargas, was against us for the final run along the shore of Calmus Passage, so we cut inside the line of kelp to catch the back eddy, resting our paddles briefly at a small mossy cove where a sign warned, CABLE, NO ANCHORAGE. Upon reaching Eby Rock, the mussel- and kelp-encrusted navigation tower marking the northwest corner of Vargas, we turned southwest where the current picked up a notch along the broad sweep of Dick and Jane's beach. The wave action changed: we were *outside*. With no kelp to protect us, it took a sprint to reach the south end. I checked my watch: just under two hours.

Mel had arrived already, his vintage aluminum runabout pulled up on rollers above the tideline on the next beach over. He had a cat-like quality I'd not noticed in the city. The acreage he owned was embedded in the Vargas Island Provincial Park, land he had purchased from a descendant of a homesteader some thirty years before.

"Homesteader?" we asked.

"Some English immigrants took up farming on plots of pre-empted land here in the early 1900s. They didn't last long. The Port Alberni folks I bought the land from had never even seen it."

Thirty thousand, he had paid back in the mid-'70s. At the time, the only other occupant was a fellow hippie, Phil, a carver, who lived on the beach in a teepee with his partner and son. Dismayed that Mel had gone to the dark side and actually purchased land, Phil moved and built a cabin behind a secluded cove on Flores, where he still lived.

Mel's beach was a half-kilometre crescent of steep sand and gravel backed by piled driftwood logs, facing northwest like ours. It had its own islet near shore as protection and, visible above the tideline, a length of wooden fence and a PLEASE RESPECT OUR PRIVACY sign. Mel started the tour at the southern extremity of his land, about a quarter of the way down. There, tucked away behind the logs and salal, was a tiny one-room cabin with a wood stove, a little gas cooker, a bench bed with no mattress, and a large window that looked out into forest gloom, once ocean view. Moss and a small forest of seedlings sprouted from the shake roof.

"This one is actually on park land," Mel confessed. "They resurveyed the park after the cabin was built, then they changed the boundary. Someday I'll get around to moving it."

A notice on the door said it was slated for demolition. ENTERING PROHIBITED; signed BC Parks. But as Mel said, "They used all their money on helicopters for demolishing the bridges on the trail from the Vargas Inn to Ahous, just so they wouldn't have to maintain them. So I still use this as a guest cabin." He shrugged. "We just have to keep the salal around it so it's not obvious from the beach."

The Vargas Island Provincial Park Reserve, dedicated in 1995, included the western half of the island except for Mel's land and, just south of it, another, much larger uninhabited chunk owned by Louisiana Joe. There was an Indigenous Reserve, also uninhabited, at the south end of Ahous Bay. (The east side of the island, aside from the Keltsmaht Reserves at Yarksis and Moser Point, was largely in private hands.) The whole of Vargas Island, meanwhile, fit within Ahousaht First Nation unceded traditional territory.

Mel walked us back to an open area to his sun-bleached, barn-sized workshop built on an ancient midden. We dragged open the doors: a six-metre industrial propane tank dominated the space. Mel had planned to use this for his glass art, but life intervened. His stepdaughter died. Mel pulled her photograph out of his wallet: a smiling redhead, fourteen. Things fell apart with his first wife, a potter, whose potter's wheel was still up in the rafters. And his new wife, well . . .

So there the tank sat on steel wheels like a huge, menacing silver pig, capable of demolishing the entire north end of the island if ignited.

Mel's workshop had no locks but one of several workbenches lifted up cunningly to reveal a collection of vintage hand tools and a modern chainsaw. Behind a stack of lumber, he had hidden a weed-whacker and a timber jack. There were old posters on the walls, a few tulip chairs from the '60s, and junk from a hundred abandoned maintenance projects cluttering the benches. Pyramids of sawdust from termite colonies in the rafters piled up like hourglass sand counting off the time till the beams gave way.

A walled, fallow garden to the side of the workshop cried out for care. Near it stood the wooden skeleton of a greenhouse, glass askew, years of tall grass dried and fallen with spring shoots pushing through.

Almost a hundred metres back from the beach, we came to Mel's house, a square cedar-shake watchtower, three storeys high. It had an enclosed front porch, blue-trimmed windows, and a vaguely Tibetan look. The tower had once offered a view of the sea but vigorous second growth meant it now had a view of trees only. It stood uncomfortably close to a massive hemlock. Mel said its roots moved the house when the wind blew.

Mel's tower.

"It was supposed to be temporary accommodation while I built a proper house on the point," he said wistfully.

There were the remains of a second greenhouse alongside. Mel pointed to salal bushes beyond a grassed area: "I used to have a little pond over there. We could hear the frogs at night."

The tower's bottom tier had a floor made entirely of loose white shells. Stairs at the back led to a locked trap door. Eventually we would get to see the tiers above, but this day we simply proceeded across the wooden porch and down to a path leading back to our beach across the peninsula. Cobber had been following us closely all this time. Now, he was distracted by mysterious scents along the way.

"Any cougars around here?" I asked.

"There used to be, but none since the deer disappeared," Mel said. "Wolves, though. Lots of wolves."

"Maybe that's what got Cobber's attention."

We knew about the wolves. Dawson had told our crew just weeks before about a recent summer when a kayaker who'd been sleeping under the stars had his head, back, and hands chewed up by a wolf at precisely the spot we'd set our tents—at the north end of our beach.[2] Fifty stitches needed to close cuts to a kayaker's scalp; two habituated wolves shot by conservation officers.

Dappled light filtered through the old-growth canopy. As we emerged on what I was already calling Our Beach, Bea gasped: "Wow," she said. "I see what you meant."

Cobber trotted more freely alongside as we made our way toward the house.

"There is a big lagoon that forms here in summer," Mel said, pointing to the mid-beach.

Up the corduroy path and there was our new home, in all its weathered splendour.

I am not sure where we started—there was so much to discuss—but over the next hours, Mel filled us in on everything from previous occupants, to water sources, to secret storage spaces, and to the discreet location of a fine, classic outhouse perched at the edge of the four-metre drop. It even had a crescent moon cut into the door and was slightly north of his property line.

"Another surveying mishap," Mel said with a chuckle. "So you get to shit in the park."

The big story was of surfer Dick and gardener Jane. They had built the place in the '80s, at Mel's invitation. He'd found them constructing a shack on what was then Crown land at the north end of the beach and admired their work. He offered a spot to build on his land. The arrangement worked well. Dick did carpentry jobs in town and made barrel wood stoves out of old truck wheels, hence the metal discards behind the workshop. He and Jane sculpted birds and tended crops, including corn, on the beach. They stayed for close to a decade, then moved to a tiny community way up the coast.

"I've heard from a couple of kayak guides that Dick was pretty hostile to visitors," I said. "One said his clients walked a bit close to Dick's boathouse and this wild looking guy appeared with an AR-15 over his shoulder: 'Where do you think you're going?'"

Survival of the mutant.

Mel's landing.

"'Just going for a walk.'

"'Keep walking.'

"Another, seeing Dick returning home with a salmon, ran up enthusiastically: 'Wow! That's a beauty. Where did you get that?'

"'Fuck off!'

"There was also the story of the camper and his girlfriend who woke up to find a naked man chainsawing a log beside their tent."

"Oh," Mel said with a little smile, "that might have been me."

A Tofino local had moved in part-time for a year or two after Dick and Jane left; then came Ed and Dorothy, who stayed eight years, on and off. When Dorothy died suddenly during a visit to Victoria, Ed could not face living on Vargas alone. Friends came to move their things out for him. Ed and Dorothy apparently believed that such remote dwellings should be encouraged to return to nature, which may explain the overgrown condition of the place when we arrived. It had been a year since her death.

Mel explained that he came to Vargas once or twice a year, usually for a week in the summer, to fix winter damage, cut his lawn "so the place looks lived in," and tend to his beloved topiary bushes by the walled garden.

We accompanied Mel back to his beach when time came for him to leave. He'd shown us roughly where Dick had dug a well behind our place, and, just behind his own workshop, he pointed to a tap coming out of the ground, covered with a plastic bag.

"I had a dowser find this spot for me," he said. "Keep an eye on this, I don't want it messed with. Kayakers used to take water from it and leave the valves open so seawater contaminated the fresh."

We helped Mel roll his runabout back down to the water's edge.

"A sweet landing spot," I said.

"It's not always like this. The beach on your side is often better, in close to the rocks. I got caught out once on my way in from town with all the cash from my marijuana crop—total chaos, boat upside down, fifty-dollar bills floating around everywhere, and a kid trapped under the boat. We saved the kid but lost the cash."

With the sound of Mel's outboard fading into the distance, we walked the length of our beach so Bea, and Cobber, could take in the full measure of it: a kilometre long, almost two hundred metres wide at low tide, and unusual in that it was convex as it stretched toward the shallow sandbar that almost reached Burgess

Islet at extreme low tide. A late dusting of snow still capped the Strathcona peaks behind McKay Island to the north. The beach was not quite as flat as I had seen it earlier that season, but still had that primal openness to sky, sea, and distant land masses, with a dozen islands gracing the middle distance.

We checked out the main BC Parks campsite, built on a sandy terrace mid-beach, and walked a short distance up the river at the boundary of Mel's property. It was flowing fast through a log-jam, where it emerged from the forest. Upstream vegetation had been "burned" by salt water for several hundred metres.

Later, after a thorough look around the house, we did an inventory of what we would need to get started over the summer and fall, and what to bring with us next time. The plan was to move in before Christmas. We locked the back door from the inside and put a little padlock on the front as we pulled it closed.

Back home in Vancouver, Bea let go any further pretense of misgivings and set to work making lists. She is good at that. The first order of business was letting the kids know about our find on Vargas. We emailed, visualizing the likely reaction at the other end: a twirling "Loco!" finger about the ear and two broad smiles. Olympia and Dylan were in Thailand, crewing together on a billionaire's yacht. We had visited them on the boat the previous year for a week's cruising through the Andaman Islands. This visit was also in order to meet Captain Les, who had become Olympia's mate.

They laughed, of course. We promised to send details and keep them posted on our progress, and they of theirs, as they would soon be heading offshore, Africa bound.

The call to my old mum in New Zealand went surprisingly well. She knew we'd been searching for such a place and had even gone looking for one on the Coromandel Peninsula, not far from her native Thames in the country's North Island. She reminded me of my discovery, as a twenty-four-year-old, of a particular dream house I had hoped to buy, without any funds, at the entrance to Pelorus Sound on the South Island. It was an abandoned Second World War naval gun emplacement, its concrete bunker sixty metres up a hillside with a six-metre-high entrance and a three-hundred-degree view over Cook Strait. Seven thousand dollars, it would have cost.

To the left, McKay Island guards the entrance to Millar Channel, the inside route to Hot Springs Cove.

Ten years later, Bea and I had jointly fixated on Castle Island lighthouse in the Bahamas. It had a dazzling white octagonal structure at the summit, with windows facing every point of the compass.

"Oh, that sounds almost reasonable," Mum said about this latest plan. "You'll need another wood cookstove like the one you had on the mountain, I imagine. I'll shout you that." She figured the place would need a heart replacement, and as it turned out, she was flush with cash, having just sold the family home in Auckland.

For Bea there was no issue.

MY PARENTS WERE NOT alive to express reservations, and in any event, cabin living was a respected tradition in my family. Each of my grandfathers—was it in the 1930s?—had built their young a refuge away from town. One was lakefront, made of logs and fieldstones; the other of plank and shakes in a woodland. My parents had wed in the first; the second was where I had last seen them together. There was a natural fit. Bea-by-the-sea it would be.

Home to us currently was an apartment at our friend Pia's place, a big yellow house on Vancouver's Kits Point. During the previous six years, we'd gone from a flat in Moscow to an ancient farm estate in Tuscany, then to an apartment in Madrid big enough for us four plus two young friends who were then on a gap year. Mostly we had followed the kids' interests: for Olympia, ballet; for Dylan, flamenco guitar. We had returned via Toronto, where we scrambled to replenish our coffers after blowing much of what selling the mountain cabin and its acre of land had brought us.

From our place on Kits Point, there was only a short walk to Cobber's doggy park by the Planetarium, and a short walk for us to get to our respective jobs: Bea at the Francophone Cultural Centre, where she saw to member services and a small library, and me on a low-key, part-time consulting gig at a kayak-and-dive store. It had its perks in that it helped me renew business acquaintances, particularly with Craig, seller of inflatables in the shop next door. Spare moments saw me there, prodding the tubes of new RIBs, sniffing glue, oil, and gasoline—heresy for a kayaker.

My schedule was more flexible than Bea's. There was a seasonal character to her job: a festival and children's camp in summer, language class registrations and membership drive in the fall, and preparations for the Christmas market. I'd be doing most summer trips to Vargas; she would join me on long weekends and for at least a week's holiday.

I was particularly looking forward to the diving. For almost forty years it had been my greatest passion after kayaking. At first just snorkelling around coral reefs in tropical waters then free-diving commercially for crayfish in New Zealand, I'd moved on to a full commercial ticket in the '70s, logging dives on oil rigs in the North Sea and on London's massive Thames Barrier Project before, less gloriously, turning to geoduck and abalone harvesting when we'd first come to BC after the Caribbean trip. I still fancied myself as a free-diver, so moving to Clayoquot Sound was an excuse to buy the free-diving wetsuit of my dreams.

The suit, apart from being expensive, was as flexible as a surgical glove and thin compared to the wetsuits I was used to as a commercial diver, with a clammy layer against the skin. It required liquid soap or hair conditioner as a lubricant to get into it, the sales rep said. I also bought metre-long free-diving fins and low-volume goggles that would reduce the squeeze around my eyes once I sank below fifteen metres. I was planning to show those sea lions a thing or two as I reverted to merman, spearing fish and collecting delicacies for the larder.

Men's large off the shelf generally fits me nicely with clothing, so I decided against trying the suit on in the dive shop. I figured I'd do that in the privacy of home.

The rep shrugged. It saved him time too.

"Just be sure to try the top and bottom separately if you're not using soap," he cautioned. "It can be sticky when the two surfaces touch."

Back in our apartment, I laid my new acquisition admiringly on the bed. The Farmer John went on easily and I wondered at all the fuss. It did not require any lubricant and fit like a second skin, though it was disconcerting the way it emphasized my fifty-nine-year-old belly.

I picked up the top. It felt like a living thing as I rolled it back like a large black condom at the waist. I pushed my arms easily into the sleeves, pulled it over my head then rolled the body part down. The moment the top rolled out over the upper part of the Farmer John, the two parts bonded with the top only half on. My arms were held firmly above my head while my face was stuck around the spot where my chest should have been.

The rep had been right about two things: it was a very warm suit, and it was amazing how those parts stuck together. In fact, I could neither pull the suit on, nor get it off. It occurred to me that I might need help to avoid suffocation.

Further complicating the situation were two old rotator-cuff shoulder injuries that made it painful to even hold my arms up, much less wrestle with the suit. I was hurting. The clammy material formed a much-too-effective seal around my face, I found. I managed to reach down with my left (best shoulder) hand and briefly pull the stretch material away from my face. This gained me a lungful of fresh air. It snapped back against my flushed cheeks. I fought back a rising panic and considered my options.

I was by now stewing hot. I imagined Bea coming home from work and finding me suffocated on the floor in a wetsuit that I'd just paid over a thousand for. She would have trouble keeping a straight face at my funeral.

Yep, I was going to need help, but how? I thought of phoning her at work, but even if I could find the phone before passing out, I would have been unable to see to dial her number…

Pia wasn't home. Darn. The option of stumbling blindly out onto the street to get some passerby to help did not exactly appeal. I mean, how do you ask a stranger you can't even see to help you off with a rubber suit?

Fresh air was once again becoming a pressing issue. I sank to my knees in the middle of the room, grasping the stretchy fabric around my nose and pulling it clear of my face for another gulp of air.

With a rising sense of desperation, I reached back behind my head as far as my ridiculous shoulders would allow and dug my fingers into the suit—then with all my strength, I hauled on the material. It stretched like a rubber band but remained stuck fast to the Farmer John. I pulled it clear of my face again and gasped another lungful of air, then resigning myself to tearing the suit in two, reached both hands as far as I could down my back and started to finger walk the fabric into a bunch around my neck.

Ignoring the pain in my shoulders, I focused all my strength into my fingers and slowly, slowly the jacket yielded against the Farmer John. Eventually my marching fingers reached the hem and with one violent movement I yanked my head clear and fell back against the bed.

As Bea put it: "Lubricate or die!"

MY FIRST trip back to Vargas was to move tools and some cooking basics into the cabin and start clearing the salal and alder that pressed against the house. I found paddling the heavily-loaded double without Bea a mighty grunt. Rounding the corner by Eby Rock, I spotted a party of twenty or so young people on the beach. A Crayola set of kayaks were pulled over logs beside a cluster of tents and some tarps. Smoke drifted from a beach fire. They watched as I inched my way against the current and, when I came ashore, were there to help carry everything up the beach. They were from Vanier High in Courtenay and this was their annual wilderness trip for graduating students, a week-long adventure. It was a great introduction to our first "regulars," and soon I knew their leaders by name. They even had a meteorologist volunteer.

My new chainsaw fired up and ten-metre alders dropped like scythed wheat, exposing what had, until many years before, been lawn. I dragged the branches onto the beach and put a match to them. The fire burned as long as I was there.

In the midst of a thicket of salal surrounded by young cedar, I found a framed rectangle that marked the outline of a vegetable garden, now overwhelmed. I cut the salal back, pulled the roots, and exposed surprisingly good soil. Normally cedar roots invade gardens, but someone had dug out all the soil and double-lined the hole with a tarp before replacing the enriched dirt. I'd bring out seeds and starters next visit.

That first trip held rewards of another kind. Aside from the dive suit, I had invested in a decent array of fishing gear. Mel had described casting off the beach and catching salmon in late spring and summer, a claim I viewed with some skepticism. He also spoke of the fishing hole where Dick said he could always get salmon. Unfortunately, Mel did not know where that was. I assembled my new rod, attached a Buzz Bomb, and after a day of hard work, set out to try my luck.

The rocky outcrops book-ending our beach seemed the obvious place to start. The area off the rocks at our (south) end, however, was choked with kelp, so I headed to the northern

Fish hanging on beach stump.

opposite It was true: casting for salmon right off the beach.

outcrop, wading into the water up to my knees and casting out toward the sandbar as I went. After just a few casts, the line went taut, the rod bent, and the reel whizzed.

I could scarcely believe it. Each in our own ways, both fish and I were hooked. I never considered myself a particularly addictive personality, but this salmon fishing was something else. One *whizz* and I got it. It was a brief but fierce battle that ended with me walking out of the water dragging a beautiful, wildly flapping coho.

Subsequent trips out were easier, but the easiest and fastest of them all came from a serendipitous encounter at work with Peter the pilot.

Peter flew commercial aircraft but he also had his own small plane and a special interest in landing it on remote beaches. He had in his possession the charts left behind by artist Toni Onley, who had famously flown, before a recent, final crash in the Fraser

River, all over the province—including Ahous Bay—to paint landscape and seascape.

Bea, the kids, and I had once come across Onley at Montague Harbour on Galiano Island, without knowing who he was. Light amphibious aircraft lands, putters up to the foreshore, and man with wooden box descends, sets up easel, paints, then departs within the hour. We'd had his *Wilderness—The Choice* poster on our wall until it fell apart.[3]

"I've often wondered about that beach," Peter said of Dick and Jane's, "but I didn't know if the sand was firm enough to land. Toni's charts didn't say anything about it."

"It's firm at low tide," I assured him. "Just keep to seaward of the lagoon."

"Should we go have a look?" he asked.

He picked me up in his truck and we drove to Boundary Bay airport. His plane was kit-built, styled after a Spitfire, with low wings, two seats one behind the other, and a disconcerting row of fake bullet holes along the fuselage. Also disconcerting was the wriggling required to get into the narrow seat, crowded by protruding aluminum frame parts like the inside of a mechanical grinder.

I love flying in small planes and this one was tiny. It bounced along the air waves like a butterfly. We flew painfully close to the nightmare scene of Vancouver Island mountainsides shorn of trees and scarred by appalling landslides. For the first time, I was able to look down and see the "green corridors" left along the roadside to trick Tofino's Winnebago tourists into thinking the area was still somewhat pristine.

We did a low pass over our beach. It was a good low tide and the sand was clear of driftwood and kelp. Smoke from a campfire gave wind direction and strength as it floated away gently to the southeast. I could hear Peter winding down the wheels. They locked in place.

We skimmed the rocky finger that pointed to Eby Rock, then the wheels touched hard sand between lagoon and sea. The little plane ran smoothly to the south end of the beach then veered up toward the cabin.

On viewing the place and hearing we'd be getting a generator, Peter said, "Could you use a freezer? I've got a decent used one you can have."

The easy way in.

We hadn't thought of that one but, yes, the fish—we could freeze the fish. And ice for the Cuba Libres, and ice cream. We'd set it up in the workshop, against the back wall. It would only need to be run a few hours each night to freeze. All we had to do was get it there.

On the priority list was the building of a vestibule on the garden side of the house, off the sunroom. We knew enough about living in rain country to know how useful it was to have a place to remove wet boots and clothing before putting on slippers and entering the house. The handsome, heavy door between kitchen and sunroom we would move to vestibule outside-door position, which made particular sense as it had a small *Who's there?* window. The existing, flimsier back door could stay put as an inside door.

The opened passage from kitchen to sunroom would, we felt, help wood stove heat reach the latter and brightness reach the former—making both rooms friendlier. The sunroom was shaping up to be the room of choice, the one for feasting, reading, and lounging, but for now it looked raw and unfinished, with a floor that sweated moisture on certain days and kicked up dust on others.

As well as drippy raingear and muddy boots, the vestibule would accommodate an icebox, with blocks of ice brought from Tofino until the promised freezer arrived. We'd also need a properly set-up barrel for rainwater with a feed from the roof as the well supply was disappointingly brackish and the pipeline blocked.

I'd found the well in a heavily overgrown area on high ground above the cabin. It had a rotting wooden lid that would have provided a nasty surprise for anyone stepping on it. The shaft was lined with mossy cedar planks and was home to a happy red-legged frog. The water looked clear but smelled of swamp, only good for watering the garden should that ever be necessary.

In July, Deakins paddled out to help build the vestibule and stayed a week to do some clearing as well. It felt good to have this friend of thirty years hammering alongside and dragging brush to the beach fire. A retired professor, he was struggling with his tome about the meaning of life. The change of scenery helped, and it was surprising how often he became engaged in philosophical discussions with kayakers camped on the beach.

Kayakers arrived solo and in pods. Our beach was a convenient stopover on the way to Hot Springs Cove for late starters from

A leadership training group.

Our grumpy neighbour
on Burgess Islet.

JULY 19, 1:00 AM. I am alone
on Vargas, sleeping. A tremor
wakes me. I sit up and time it:
thirty seconds. Then I go back
to sleep. It was, I find out later,
a 6.4 magnitude earthquake
eighty kilometres offshore.

Tofino. It was the point where a decision had to be made to go up the dramatic outside of Flores, with its hazardous Rafael Point and exposed shoreline, or take the quieter inside route along Millar Channel. A number of kayakers had come to grief on the exposed coast in recent years so if they had to ask, we'd advise the safer route.

I hooked a gas bottle to the two-ring burner and presto: we had tea. Deakins, an Englishman, loved his tea with gingersnaps or digestives. So long as there was tea and biscuits, he would work all day. But we didn't. From the front porch, we often sat in the newly arrived Adirondack chairs, conscious we were just the latest in a line of people who had sat there before us.

Deakins set up his 20x scope on its tripod so we could view the passing parade while reclining. Whale-watching boats whizzed by to find the gentle cetaceans the spotting plane had just flagged. Then there was the *Leviathan II*: a ridiculous shallow-draft, top-heavy monstrosity that kicked up a rooster-tail fifteen metres long. It roared past once or twice a day with tourists by the busload.

Sport fishing boats, sometimes dozens of them, motored around in circles right off our beach. We could see rods bent like bows and flashing silver as they hauled salmon from the school gathering off Burgess, waiting for some mysterious signal to go upriver to spawn. It was known as one of the best coho and spring hotspots on the West Coast.

Burgess Islet was also home to a family of bald eagles with two stick nests visible from the porch. Most times, we could see one or two eagles on bare branches waiting for action below.

One morning, Deakins gave a whoop of delight. He'd witnessed an osprey drop suddenly into the surf, re-emerging with a small fish. A shiver and a shake and it was off with one of the Burgess eagles hot on its tail. A raven joined in, tight on the eagle's tail. Up and up they went. As the eagle drew closer, the osprey released the fish. The eagle rolled after it, then, just as it was about to catch it, the raven had it by the tail feathers. There was a squawk and the fish fell back into the sea. Everyone went back to where they were.

IN ANOTHER of those serendipitous encounters, a New Zealand "bloke" in his mid-thirties walked into the shop while I was working the floor. Glenn had just arrived in Vancouver on leave from work as an administrator in Micronesia. Within a few minutes, I

An early trip in.

heard myself offering him a place to stay on Vargas. That weekend he and I kayaked out to the island. He was right at home and became our first house-sitter for a couple of weeks.

Other friends came to help, motoring in with Marcel, a herring skiff operator who'd been recommended to us and whose services we would be needing for our big stuff. Marcel was a salvager with experience pulling out the odd wrecked plane from the big beach at Ahous when they hit soft sand or worse. He and his wife Joanna—a kayak author whose book *Paddling through Time* Bea had only just bought as part of our new library—lived on a floathouse in Tofino harbour, part of a dockside community near Strawberry Island.

By the time Bea took her holiday week, the big jobs remaining on the summer's to-do list were the floor of the sunroom and clearing out the mezzanine.

The sunroom floor was a pig of a job. The object was to make the interstices between cedar blocks impervious so it could be kept dry and clean. This required digging and sweeping out all the loose fill to a depth of several inches, replacing it with cement, then sprinkling smooth pebbles back in for a natural look. Next came the scrubbing and sealing of the cedar blocks. The job took several days and a fair amount of knuckle skin, but was worth the effort. We even touched up the kitchen floor for good measure.

Next, Bea took on the mezzanine and I went fishing—to each their own. She tossed a lot of random paper and cardboard trash out, shoving it down through a ladder-access gap in the parapet into the sunroom, and from there to the beach fire.

AMONGST ALL THE JUNK and debris, I found Ed and Dorothy's move-in list, showing the things they had come with, detailed in small handwriting. A different box yielded an astonishing variety of plant labels handwritten on Popsicle sticks, likely dating back to Jane. On an earlier trip, I had come across a hair band made of braided fabric, a pair of good leather loafers just my size, and a wide-brimmed sun hat. I left them untouched. Some day I might wear them.

There is something cathartic about clearing land around a neglected dwelling, like rolling back time. And somehow, the more we cleared, the more intrigued we became by what lay beyond. This is how, after a network of clogged ditches had been revealed and cleared to drain the sphagnum swamp and skunk-cabbage plantation, we discovered an archery target—a substantial wood-framed structure holding blocks of polystyrene wrapped in hemp cloth.

We pushed a little farther into salal near the edge of the outhouse bank and discovered a chest-high raised garden with a roller top that, with the replacement of a few struts, some refreshed soil, and new plastic sheeting, would provide an excellent greenhouse. There was a cold frame on a small cedar table alongside, ready for nursing seeds. Meanwhile, the rotting kelp I had dug into the two garden plots uncovered earlier in the season was having good effect. Cabbage and carrot plantings were taking well, and I added more pellets to deal with the giant banana slugs that apparently had genetic memory for young cabbage plants.

Back in Vancouver, I pestered Bea to make the move early. In the end, she relented and agreed we'd head to Vargas at the end of summer, in a month's time, rather than waiting till mid-winter. It proved to be a good move but giving notice was, shall we say, *délicat*, and Bea's boss Pierre was in a right tizzy over it. Soon enough, however, the right replacement was found and Bea felt free to go.

From that point on, everything began to accelerate in earnest and every list begat two more. We found new tenants for Pia, new owners for our excess furniture, and new ways to underestimate costs and obstacles. Cobber, sensing another move was pending, followed us around constantly. He knew something serious was up when we began packing boxes.

We bought the generator in Vancouver and set off for a last summer trip to Tofino. We ordered the wood stove in Parksville on our way through in Deakins's old Mazda, now being borrowed for the last time. There was much to do in Tofino, after which we'd nip out to Vargas once again to check on the house and drop off what would fit in the big kayak, one of several we had stored on Dorothy's rental racks in Tofino. Dorothy owned and ran the local kayak/bookshop combo, Tofino Sea Kayaking, and its associated bed and breakfast on the waterfront.

The stove we chose was forest green enamel with a shelf on one side. An Irish import, it would be delivered to our friends Cindy and Dave in Tofino. Dave had a construction company with

Sea rocket patch.

a hefty enough truck to get it to the dock, and a team of workers to help load the 350-kilogram beast into Marcel's skiff.

Bea reread the to-do list out loud as we turned right at the Tofino/Ucluelet junction.

"**GET POST OFFICE BOX;** open bank account; see to address change for driver's licence; buy VHF radio."[4]

We gave priority to sticky buns and coffee at the Common Loaf café, where the lineup seemed not too bad and the smells irresistible. From there, it was thirty steps across the street to the post office, where we asked about a PO box and were met with an apologetic wince. A PO box, it turned out, was a big ask in this little town of too many transients and too few boxes. Friends of ours had been waiting for months but we jumped the queue because those without a street address had priority. So we left with one key each, inspected our bread-loaf-sized box, and rejoiced in our new status as Greater Tofino residents (winter population about 1,500). There was even a local name for us, "offshore people," like it was some sort of club.

Back across the street now to the only commercial bank in town, we duly checked in as new clients—using our brand new mailing address, which we had planned to use also as the new address for our drivers' licences. Not so fast: post office box numbers were not accepted for that purpose. "You need," the man said, "an address the RCMP can find you at." *A-ha*. The address on our card thus became: Dick & Jane's Beach, Vargas Island, Tofino, BC. That did the trick.

Since late spring, we'd mucked around town enough to know where to shop for what. Which, in Tofino, meant Co-op, Co-op, and Co-op: one for food, one for dry goods, one for gas. The other key place was the liquor store, hidden behind the Loaf.

Eager to head off to our RCMP address, we loaded up on a few food items, in particular the sorts of things that would pair well with the fish John might have time to catch. We headed down to the marine store to pick up our VHF radio, then to Dorothy's beach, where we slipped on our dry suits and got packing. Cobber was pleased to get out after so long in the car, though he could see what was coming.

Dan and Bonny, friends of old, came down to see us off. They too lived off the grid, on a town-facing island near Opitsaht, but they kept an office in town, right next door to Dorothy's, with a bed and cook-up facilities so they could stay put in dirty weather. Bonny had burst into Dan's life through the environmental movement. She had been thrown in jail during the War in the Woods, a fierce eco-warrior. They were now both involved with the Friends of Clayoquot Sound while running a kayak leadership school.

Dan could make a kayak dance. He had contributed to both our video series and a fresh edition of my 1980s vintage kayak manual, giving it a new chapter on a course curriculum developed jointly with Dawson, who, at the time, taught outdoor pursuits at Malaspina College (now Vancouver Island University). Our paths had intersected often over the years: he had, with our partner Christine, taught the first classes at our shop and had lived in our mountain cabin when we needed to work from town. He had known our kids as kids, and been the first to whisper that subversive word, "unschooling," in our ears. Thus, like the two Johns (Deakins and Dawson), he was deemed an uncle and was now about to be a neighbour.

Objects strapped on higgledy-piggledy after a somewhat rushed loading job, dog in, paddles out, we pushed off, making it past Eby too tired to fish, but ready to puzzle out one particular mystery—hidden storage.

We hadn't given the matter much thought over the summer but now faced a decision to leave or not leave some of our goods in the storage locker they had had to occupy, at some expense, in Vancouver. We opted to take everything with us. There was supposed to be usable dry storage in the house, if we could find it. We started to look for the sort of place someone with something to hide might think up to confound intruders.

The obvious space was under the bunk-style upholstered couches, which were built rather high, even for tall people. Then there was the space under the large built-in desk against the beach-facing window, which had a solid planked front. Neither the top nor the front hinted at any way it could be opened.

We looked closely at the vertical shakes beneath the bunk/couch, remembering Mel's mention of carefully crafted shake panels that could be removed in a counter-intuitive way to reveal storage.

Bingo!

And the reward was . . . a plastic tub of fishing lures, hooks, and rolls of nylon line. The under-desk storage remained a mystery, however, until we went outside and moved aside some water barrels. We then lifted out a panel of shakes from the outside wall and we had it: a space the width of the house and high enough to stand in.

There was also a crawl space beneath the living room once we discovered how to roll forward the heavy set of steps. There we found enamel stove pipes and fancy glass light fittings, as well as a selection of pots and pans.

Outside again, another discovery. From the north end of the front porch we saw that the gutter, made of heavy-gauge bamboo, fed down to a mossy aqueduct that in turn led into a dense thicket of salal. Half an hour's work with loppers following the aqueduct revealed two plastic reservoirs beside a large cast-iron bathtub. It was set atop one of Dick's furnace creations, a firebox with a hinged door. The rusted remains of a smokestack stood askew behind the bath, which although thick with rotting leaves appeared in good shape. The final link of the aqueduct pivoted to direct water to either bath or barrel. Bliss! We'd be having hot baths under the stars.

Still on our "To Get" list was the word *cat*. Cobber had nothing against small felines and, judging from the droppings, we'd need a mouser. So we responded to an advertisement on the Loaf notice board and made arrangements to pick one from a recent litter in Tofino. The young family we visited on our way out of town agreed to keep a kitten for us until we were ready.

By this time, it was also becoming clear we were going to need more than kayaks to live on Vargas. And, wouldn't you know it, Craig had good things in stock that I had been checking out during my lunch breaks.

We chose a three-and-a-half-metre rigid inflatable with a thirty-horsepower, four-stroke motor.

From now on, sea and
sky would set the rules.

Ibrahim, a resident. He and his
partner Fatima ruled the territory.

2

BIG MOVES

IN SEPTEMBER, OUR FINAL load of possessions was ready to move from Tofino to Vargas Island. It was also the first time we would inflate our new boat and bolt on the motor. Noel, a kayak friend, had volunteered his panel van to move everything from Vancouver and help us get out to the island. At Fourth Street dock, Cobber was having an anxiety attack as he watched Marcel's herring skiff being loaded. We three then fumbled the heavy motor onto the now plumped up inflatable, loading plastic bins of supplies till there was hardly room left for legs.

My prior experience with outboards was mostly limited to connecting fuel lines and checking oil levels, so it took longer than expected to get the new boat set up, loaded, and into the water. Operating instructions on the hand tiller consisted of two symbols, a hare and a tortoise—my kind of instructions.

A fresh northwesterly had picked up by the time we departed. Marcel drove his skiff into the chop, washing down Bea's small but carefully chosen assortment of quasi-antiques with spray. Bea and Cobber had opted to ride with Marcel rather than participate in my learning curve.

Noel rode with me. He was a soft-spoken guy and everything he did was measured. I was experimenting with the throttle, a feature I was rapidly developing a passion for. After one particularly spectacular leap off the crest of a breaking wave into the belly of the next, Noel blew the seawater off the tip of his nose and leaned across.

"Perhaps a little less of the hare and a little more of the tortoise," he suggested.

Two more trips for the woodstove and freezer and we'd be done.

Load, profile, and headwind notwithstanding, we made it to Eby Rock in half an hour. At the beach on Vargas, Marcel dropped anchor off the bow of his skiff and backed in close to the south rocks where the waves were manageable. Our belongings were hastily offloaded onto the sand then shuttled clear of the incoming tide. Noel needed to return to Vancouver promptly so took the ride back with Marcel, arranging to return later to help with projects.

Cobber meanwhile viewed the forest and the vast expanse of beach uneasily and stayed close to us. He'd seen too many moves in the past few years.

The sound of Marcel's retreating motor faded into the swish of waves. High above, a formation of geese murmured gently to one another as they migrated south along the coast . . . they had so far

to go, and us, we had just arrived. We had a hug amongst our pile of belongings, then carried everything up the beach.

As we sorted our things near the boathouse, a pair of ravens dropped onto a nearby log. We had noticed those two on previous trips and since they were clearly locals and we were about to become permanent residents in their territory, we figured we'd make friends. Bea tossed some soggy crusts but was indignant when the much larger male gobbled down his piece then chased his partner away and ate hers. Bea named them on the spot, Ibrahim and Fatima.

"Racial profiling," I chided, but the names stuck and would lead to endless conniving to ensure that, in future, Fatima always received more than her share.

Cobber and his comfort stick.
Behind, Catface Mountain.
NOEL POOLE

First to the morsel.

We moved all the furniture, furnishings, and supplies closer to their final destinations in the house, workshop, and garden. Our carrots and cabbages looked almost ready to harvest and the herb garden was thriving in the sunny window boxes. Even the grass seed had sprouted, giving the backyard a bright new look.

"This place needs a pond," I said. "We always had a pond at home in New Zealand."

"Later," said Bea.

My priority was the workshop and at last I had what I needed to finish the job. I bolted a new vice onto the workbench, unpacked and arranged the chisels, handsaws, planes, and hammers on the wall, then assembled the table saw. Next, I winched the heavily corroded old tractor out from its resting place among the salal, rolled it down the ramp, and tucked it in behind the boat shed where it could gradually dissolve into a pile of rust while it served as an anchor should a high tide threaten to wash the building away.

Our new generator fit nicely into the generator hut. It started first try and purred away gently. I connected it to the wiring that scavengers had missed and then walked around with a bag of light bulbs and screwed them into blind sockets. Gradually the old house lit up one bulb at a time, like it was being brought back from an induced coma.

Bea, meanwhile, washed down the bedraggled houseplants and unrolled the big Turkish carpet onto the living room floor. She put up some favourite paintings in the living room and a calendar in the kitchen, then set about scrubbing surfaces and finding permanent places for the contents of plastic bins. This included an expanded reference library we would need to get a better grasp of the area and our neighbours, both human and creature. There were two books about the Nuu-chah-nulth Peoples, and others about crows and ravens, trees, shorebirds, shellfish, and wolves. There was also one about a famous settler, Cougar Annie. She had lived in Hesquiaht Harbour, the upper limit of Clayoquot Sound, from 1915 to the early 1980s.

Much of what we had brought with us was detritus from previous lives... thousands of photographs, documents, tax files, and an entire bin of writing and travel journals. It all fit in the stand-up locker where most of it would remain undisturbed for a decade.

Sleep came easily that night. At peace with the move, we were lulled by the swish of waves on the beach. Both of us thrived on new beginnings.

After kayaking the Caribbean, we had been faced with the choice of living on a sailboat or in a log cabin above Vancouver. We chose the mountains, though the link to the sea remained through our business. Now, after almost twenty-five years, we were recommitting to the sea, and to each other.

I LIKED our new boat. It was just right for the job, with a deep-V aluminum hull, upswept bow for a "dry" ride, and tough UV-resistant tubes. It would have power enough to get us to Tofino in fifteen to twenty minutes fully loaded and had the space for large loads. It was also light enough for us to get it up the beach by ourselves. A set of foldaway wheels bolted to the transom helped. We

South rocks, Brabant Channel. Home.

could flop the wheels down, slip a canoe cart under the forward section, and pull the boat up the sand to the boathouse, a fifty- to two-hundred-metre stretch depending on the tide.

One day when the sea was calm with just a light surf, we pulled on dry suits and life jackets, small waterproof VHF radios in our pockets, and set off for an exploratory tour. As we passed Eby, we spotted wire wrapped around its navigation tower. Apparently a fishing boat with its outrigger spread wide had had a brush with the rock during the night.

None of the surrounding islands except Flores were inhabited, so our closest neighbours lived in the cabins across the water on Catface, a peninsula of mainland Vancouver Island. At the south-eastern tip of Catface was a bleached wood house tucked into the trees partway up a cliff of sheer rock, accessible by a wooden cat-walk from a floating dock with a drawbridge. With no boat at the dock and no smoke from the chimney, we figured no one was home.

We continued west, nosing into every cove looking for signs of habitation. There was a cabin with a battered aluminum dinghy pulled high into the bushes, but long grass showed it had not been moved that summer.

Around the corner, tucked into a pocket beach, was a cozy-looking shake house with blue windowsills. No sign of life there either.

Further on ... life: smoke drifted from two cabins. As the crow flies, they were our nearest neighbours. A cedar log was tied to the shore as salvage. A big man came to his door, took one look, and went back inside. A young man with a mop of curly hair emerged from the other, introducing himself as Sam and the big man as his dad. By this time, surf was dumping on a steep pebble beach, making conversation difficult and landing a bad idea.

We moved on toward Maaqtusiis, home of the ʕaaḥuusʔatḥ (Ahousaht) People. Near the entrance to Millar Channel a cluster of houses came into view behind a pebble beach. Dawson told of a time in the early ’70s when he and a companion, on their way to Hot Springs Cove in whitewater kayaks, landed on that beach and were overwhelmed by crowds of children touching their boats in wonder. Much had changed since then.

The approach to the Nuu-chah-nulth community was from the north, along a glassy, calm canal. Dense forest rolled to the sea on either side. We tied up at a wobbly dock beside a couple of herring skiffs. The general store was distinguished from nearby cedar shake houses by a DRINK COCA-COLA sign in the window. Like a pair of aliens in our yellow suits, we walked the aisles searching for some stove fittings I needed. The place was deserted except for a woman in a long dress chatting to the cashier. Neither paid attention to us.

The store did not have what I sought, so we bought some candy and chips from a selection that took up almost half the shelf space. We knew nobody in town and the idea of wandering around like tourists did not appeal. So we simply puttered up the inlet toward a cluster of grim-looking houses behind a second dock. It was Ahousaht viewed from the other side, reminiscent of remote fishing villages I'd seen in Chile. The only sign of life was a couple of brown dogs politicking on the street. Masts from half a dozen submerged boats protruded from the shallows.

"Let's go," said Bea.

The quiet of the town and inlet was unsettling. The kids must have been in school.

At more than 2,000 members, the Ahousaht are the most populous First Nation on the west coast of Vancouver Island. More than a third live in Maaqtusiis. Two Ahousaht Hereditary Chiefs we knew of through their work: Chief Earl Maquinna George, whose book *Living on the Edge* Bea had begun reading, and Ah-in-chut Shawn Atleo, then Regional Chief of the Assembly of First Nations.[1]

Ahousaht territory had originally been small, consisting of the west coast of Vargas and the south-facing part of Catface. Their main settlement of Ahous Bay provided good sealing and whaling. In the nineteenth century, a thirteen-year war occurred, pitting the Ahousaht against their neighbours, the Otsosaht. Muskets were involved. The Otsosaht, a much larger, more powerful nation, were eventually vanquished, and the victors left Ahous Bay for the protection of Matilda Inlet, securing access to the territory's fourteen salmon rivers.

Aside from the Ahousaht/Maaqtusiis community, there are two dozen small, uninhabited Ahousaht reserves dotting the coast between the Hesquiaht and Tla-o-qui-aht First Nations' traditional territories.[2] Bartlett Island (Nu-a-suk) is among them: we could just see it from the house, large, low-lying, and mysterious.

Mel's island. To the right, on the horizon, Bartlett Island; further to the east, the distinctive tufts and sand berm on the main islet in the Whaler group.

Back the way we had come, we headed southwest toward it.

En route, we pulled into the largest of the Whaler Islets, two rocky outcrops joined by a tussock-tufted sand dune. It enjoyed some protection from ocean waves, tucked in as it was just a kilometre behind Bartlett. We had filmed there for our oceanography video because its beaches were swept on both sides by wraparound waves during a westerly blow. It was the only place we found where waves could run *along* the beach, both sides of an island at the same time. It was also of interest to the video because the worst place to land was the first place most people would go—the leeward end. There, waves collided to form pinnacles over a sand bar.

Close to where we landed, on the Flores side, wolf tracks led out of the sea to a sunny spot where the animal had rolled in the warm sand before re-entering the water at the closest point to Bartlett. Wet sand and water droplets still splattered the blades of grass where it had had a shake within the past hour.

We relaunched the boat and continued westward. Rounding Bartlett's southerly tip, we met four-metre swells. The boat felt entirely comfortable. A raft of twenty or more sea otters lay back in their bed of kelp, waving webbed feet in the air, whiskers twitching as we motored past. They were, thanks to a reintroduction scheme in the 1970s, reclaiming this stretch of coast after their near extinction the century before.

The exposed south and west side of Bartlett was a fortress of black rock, encrusted with mussels, barnacles, and golden kelp streaming in the surge like maple syrup. Tucked behind the barrier islets, a series of sandy beaches stretched for half a mile. Dozens of canoes had once been drawn up at this ancient campsite. Ashore we found no sign of old longhouses, just a tumbledown shack beneath a frayed blue tarp and a midden of empty pop cans.

WE WERE TRESPASSING. PERMISSION is required to visit, we later found out, in large part because the island, known as Nu-a-suk, is now used as a place for spiritual healing or prescribed solitary penance as meted out by the Indigenous Justice Strategy.

Flores loomed large from here: a giant bunched fist facing inland, its right thumb the Maaqtusiis peninsula, its top knuckle—Mt. Flores—almost nine hundred metres high. Alongside it, Vargas looked like a child's upturned palm.

Like Vargas, Flores has a provincial park, a wide swath along the exposed side. It takes up forty-one square kilometres—about a quarter of the total. Most of the rest is now Crown land.

We had neighbours up that way, on the open side: Phil lived somewhere between Kutcous Point and Cow Bay, within sight of his old teepee beach, and Cow Bay was home to a reclusive couple in a squat. The bay was the end point of an eleven-kilometre hiking trail from Maaqtusiis: the fabled Wild Side Trail, threading eight beaches.

I knew something of that huge, surf-swept scallop of sand through our filming trip: we'd sampled a combination of fog and swells there that had our oceanographer remark he'd never seen such seas in his thirty-year career.

All storms must end.

Moonset over the Whaler Islets.

THE COOKSTOVE and chest freezer arrived on our beach in Marcel's skiff, along with enough friends to carry them up to the house. We put the freezer in the workshop, then did a final assembly of the stove in the sunroom before grunting it into place in the kitchen and connecting the stovepipe. It was an airtight, with an oven large enough for a Christmas turkey and hot plate space for half a dozen pots at once. Bea named it Audrey in honour of my elderly mum.

Autumn sun streamed through the tall windows of the sunroom. Dave and Cindy's kids played in the sand and Cobber frolicked with their Bernese mountain puppy on the beach. Bea set up tea and cookies on a table outside and cold beers appeared. With the stove puffing its first smoke, Dave, his two-year-old son on his shoulders and puppy at his side, went for a walk along the trail to Mel's beach. On the way back, they met a wolf.

He described it as a long-legged tawny animal. It stood atop a nearby mossy mound, watching. Dave had worked caretaking an Alaskan fishing lodge and was familiar with, if not comfortable around, wolves. He stood his ground, staring the animal down, expecting it to turn and run. It didn't. Holding his son's legs with one hand, he waved the other and yelled. The wolf moved closer. That was when Dave scooped up the puppy and backed down the trail. An hour later he was still shaken.

"Someone better shoot that wolf," he said. "It's totally habituated."

Occasionally over the next few weeks we saw wolf prints on the beach. They were the size of my hand. The rear left leg was leaving a consistent drag mark, as if the animal was limping. Twice we glimpsed it in the distance, watching as I cut beach lumber. It was an elegant, rangy animal. Bea called it Amadeus. We liked knowing it was there, watching from the shadows only to vanish the next moment. Each time it came around, Cobber grew agitated but did not bark.

In time, we started to notice more wolf tracks on the beach. Visitors told stories of wolf encounters around camp. We learned that the month before the infamous attack on our beach, our friend Martin, leader of an outdoor program with ten students from a fancy private school, had been awoken by yells at four in the morning. Wolves were tearing into one of the students' tents. Arming themselves with sticks and flashlights, the group created

Sea wolf, seeing and being seen.
TIM IRVIN (BOTTOM)

A school group at Hidden beach.

enough commotion to give what proved to be a pack of seven wolves cause for pause. The reprieve was short-lived. The wolves were soon back, rushing amongst the frightened teens. Flares fired and pots banged amid much yelling while they frantically broke camp then launched into the breaking dawn. No one was hurt.

That attack occurred at Hidden beach, just a quarter mile west of Mel's beach and though Martin, one of the most experienced guides on the coast, reported the incident, he was not taken seriously by park authorities. They suggested the attack was the result of kayakers leaving food around camp. Indeed, the consensus among locals, many of whom darkly referred to kayakers as "speed bumps," seemed to have been that they deserved what they got.

None of this made sense to me since I knew the sub-species *Homo kayakensis* pretty well. As a group they were probably the most environmentally conscious of all users of Clayoquot Sound, and the program Martin was running stressed West Coast camping discipline that included caching food in bear hangs away from camp and never, *never* bringing food into tents.

We later learned that, back in their day, Dick and Jane actually fed wolves inside the house, and Mel said they often sat around in the sun with a wolf pack. He had proudly shown us a torn shirt, the result of a tug-of-war with one. This explained a good part of the problem. It was as if diminished fear of humans was being passed around.

We already had evidence that wolves swam between islands and were likely in touch with one another as the pack size changed. They are a coastal sub-species, and although sea wolves would happily take down a deer, they are not dependent on venison, and are well able to survive foraging the shoreline.

LABOUR DAY weekend had seen at least a dozen kayak groups camped on our beach. A surprising number of them were people we remembered or who remembered us. I'd walk by on my way to my fishing spot and someone would say, "Do you recognize this boat? You sold it to me in 1983. It's been a good boat."

It was a familiarity we had not expected.

After Labour Day, paddlers mostly stopped coming and whale-watching became less of a presence. The number of sport fishing boats hovering off Burgess also dropped to just the odd one or two,

left Salmon fest.

right Audrey, heart of the house.
MARLIN BAYES

looking for that salmon left behind. The result was that our island started to feel more wild and clear. The weather began to change. Wind and rain softened the footprints in the sand and beat down blackened campfire rings.

We took advantage of what remained of September's sunny days, eating the last fresh seasonal salmon, barbequed on a hibachi outside, on the old picnic table that used to live in the sunroom. We had resolved to always take special care of at least one meal a day. Usually this was lunch since we both preferred light tapas in the evenings.

The sea was generous to us. As well as salmon, it delivered several large round commercial crab traps onto the beach after a spot of rough weather. I fixed the unwanted holes with wire and attached a good length of rope with bleach-bottle floats, then set them off Mel's beach with fresh fish heads for bait. Next morning, both traps were crawling with crabs. I threw back the females and undersized, which left six big males, enough for a feast and some for the freezer. Bea worked for hours pulling the last piece of meat from the smallest leg. We dipped them in our favourite sauce (mayonnaise, lemon juice, and tomato paste), seasoned with salt and a pinch of cayenne.

Then came the rockfish. As salmon became scarce, I went further afield in the boat for bottom fish. The Shot Islets, visible from our porch, were the obvious place to start with their abundance of reefs, kelp beds, and protected sites no matter the wave direction. That first time, just moments after dropping my lure, I had a copper rockfish, then another, then a couple of starry flounder, then home.

Plover Reef, with its raucous gang of disgruntled, foul-smelling sea lions, was also a good area for ling cod, large-mouthed monsters with a formidable array of sharp teeth. The seas were uneasy, though, with unpredictable colliding waves forming pinnacles that rushed, seething onto the rock. No place to hang around.

Though in terms of food we were managing nicely, two pressing household issues remained.

We fixed the hot-tub chimney so we could sit in the bath without passing out from smoke. That meant extending the chimney pipe two metres above our heads. The bath proved to be a little tight for two, but we both squeezed in, only to leap out and retrieve a mat to sit on—we'd burned our bums. Raindrops splashed into our Dubonnet cocktails as steam swirled. This now looked quite workable.

As for our continuing mouse problem, time soon came to pick up our kitten from where she lived in a Tofino garage. The folks there had already named her Vargas. I picked the tiny thing up and brought her back in a cardboard box, bouncing around in the boat. We opened the box inside the house. Bea was ecstatic. Of all the kittens in the litter, this had been her secret first choice. She was wearing one of those mottled rabbit-fur coats popular with teenage girls—a tortoiseshell.

"Shame about that crooked tail. They said she was born that way."

The kitten made a raspy noise. Cobber sniffed her. She bristled and made that noise again. But soon they were friends, happy enough to share the same end of the couch.

NEAR THE equinox, Olympia blew in from Madagascar like a tropical squall. Her eyes were Wedgwood blue. She was tanned and freckled, her hair a mass of sun-bleached curls.

After Thailand, the yacht Olympia and Dylan were crewing on had crossed the Indian Ocean then motored north to Dubai for

Clockwise from top left: Mel's
guest cabin; the pom-pom tree;
Little Baja at low tide; and
Olympia on Dunes beach.

repairs, then south to Madagascar. There, the kids had signed off. Dyl opted to hang around and crew on a charter sailboat for a few weeks, but Olympia was ready for home cooking.

"Les is shipping my cat over from Kenya next month," she said. "Oh, and by the way, I invited Les for Christmas."

It was fun showing her around. By then, we had somewhat figured out the lay of the land. She was predictably enchanted by Mel's tiny guest cabin, and immediately started collecting berries and chanterelles in places we had never looked. At the far end of Mel's beach, we picked up the trail to the west-facing beaches—a trail in use for hundreds of years, first by the Ahousaht People, with camps dotted along its length, then by those unfortunate English settlers attracted here by over-ambitious promoters.

The settlements were a failure in no small part because the land was unsuitable for farming, but the First World War and the flu pandemic of 1918–19 had not helped. The trail, though currently ill-maintained, had long offered shipwrecked mariners a way to walk out to the sheltered eastern side of Vargas.

We had taken machetes and loppers with us, opening the path as we went, crawling under and scrambling over giant blowdowns. There had been selective logging here long ago, with mossy stumps standing like giant tombstones. The peninsula between Mel's beach and the first big sand beach, known to surfers and kayakers as Little Baja, was through the land owned by Louisiana Joe—an eye surgeon from New Orleans. He and his ex-wife had purchased over forty hectares of the abandoned pre-empted land. It included a forest of old-growth giants and the snug cove of Hidden beach, totally protected by a barrier of small islands, reefs, and kelp beds.

We came out of the forest into a fringe of wind-sculpted dwarfed shore pines leading to a grand rocky promontory. The view demanded attention. We sat, swigging from a shared water bottle. To the north we could see the coastline stretch from Flores all the way to Hesquiaht. Bartlett, Blunden, and several small islets filled in the sweep to the west and south. Swells broke at our feet sending spray into the air and shivers through the rock we sat on. A corroded winch, half hidden by salal, awaited materials for Louisiana Joe's dream house. He had cleared a house site but that is where it stopped.

"What's with the cloud on the horizon?" Olympia asked.

"It's sea fog," I said. "By the feel of the wind, it could be coming our way."

Most of the year, sea fog lurked far offshore at the edge of the banks where cool air above a cold current from the north meets warm air above the banks. There it sat until, during the heat of late July, August ("Fogust" in the vernacular), and early September, hot air rising in the interior of BC drew fog into coastal inlets. Many unwary mariners, watching their fishing rods on a clear sunny day, could suddenly face thirty knots of wind and fifty metres visibility. Terrifying. In the forest, fog condensed on needles and lichen, dripping constantly so even during "good weather" the mossy floor was damp—perfect for mushrooms.

We rock-hopped down to the smooth sand of Little Baja and took off our shoes.

"It's hard to imagine anyone going hungry here," Olympia said. "What with all those mussels, and these!" She picked up the shell of a razor clam.

We followed the high tide line, checking out the flotsam for items of interest.

"Have you found any Japanese glass balls yet?" she asked.

"Haven't looked," I confessed.

"This used to be called Hopkins Beach, after one of the settlers," Bea said, quoting from something she'd read. "The next one, the surfers call Dunes. And there's a Monks Lake in behind it. Look." She produced an aerial photograph from her daypack and spread it on a log.

We walked past a beach reef so encrusted with mussels and barnacles there was hardly any rock visible at sea level. Dunes beach was wide, with a lagoon in close against a massive drift of sand that blew into forest. Windblown sand stung our feet as it snaked across a rapidly drying beach. At its southern end, a crab float hung from a dead tree, marking the resumption of the trail. Here, it morphed into a tunnel beneath wind-sculpted trees and eventually opened into a dark, tranquil forest. Wind sighed softly in the treetops.

Fingers beach, our destination for the day, consisted of three tight little coves facing Ahous Bay. They were a favourite of kayakers, with campsites in open forest and a stream of clear water running over rock. I searched the beach at Ahous through binoculars for signs of aircraft . . . nothing. I guessed it looked exactly as it had a thousand years ago.

Bea volunteered that for a brief time during homesteader days, a Mr. and Mrs. Cleland had enjoyed horse and cart rides along that stretch of sand. It was their home, known then as Open Beach.

Someday, no doubt, we would walk that last bit of coastal trail to the near end of Ahous, timing the tide so we could wade across its wide lagoon—a crab nursery—to the main stretch of surf-lined beach. Bea and I had camped at Ahous Bay together during video days, and she had hiked the three-kilometre telegraph trail to and from the Vargas Island Inn.

A LOVELY WALK IT had been, though eerily silent—not a breath of wind ruffling the scant bog vegetation of sedge, California myrtle, and stunted shore pine, not a bird song along the rough corduroy trail interrupted by deep mud holes where the bridges had been. The aerial photo I'd carried, a handout from the Inn, showed strange semi-circular ridges halfway along, mirroring the curve of the beach; sand berms indicating the island's gradual rise, driven by plate tectonics.

There was mystery here, a sense of arrested time. The old inn had first appeared to me like a vision, emerging as it had from deep fog on the night of our arrival from Tofino, a two-storey Tudor-style house, heavy-timbered and startlingly incongruous in its New World setting. I had not known about the English settlers then, nor that Neil's forebear had been a promoter in the land pre-emption scheme.

The house referred to as the Manor was surrounded by a scattering of plain cedar cabins and had a communal kitchen perfect for outdoor groups. There was running water and solar power for lights.

For our visit, Neil had kindly provided from his crab traps, though mostly he and Marilyn kept to their own quarters a little away from guests.

The two had been there since the 1970s, operating a sawmill for a time, raising children. Their stretch of beach, Suffolk Bay, had once been home to a lively First World War bride whose memoir, *Lone Cone*, Bonny had given me to read as we moved to Vargas. The property faced east toward Meares Island and the mountains of

Bliss.

Opposite Best buddies, Vargas and Trim.

Strathcona Park, set between two Reserves once occupied by the qiɬcmaʔatḥ (Keltsmaht) People.

Besides Neil and Marilyn, we knew of only one set of neighbours on Vargas, a doctor/fisher and his wife who were there part-time. There was a discreet cabin at the island's southern end, once occupied by a visiting ethnobotanist.

Wickaninnish Island, just to the south across a turbulent channel, had several houses, one or two with year-round residents.

OLYMPIA SOON took up temporary quarters in Tofino, hosted by Cindy and Dave whom she had known since childhood. She did odd jobs in town—of the kind local workers tended to vacate as soon as surf was up—and awaited her cat.

Trim arrived in a fancy travel box. She had with her a vaccination certificate from Thailand, a health certificate (in French) from Antananarivo, an authorization from Mombasa, a vet clearance from Frankfurt, and release papers from Vancouver airport. She was delirious with purrs when she recognized Olympia at the terminal. A sleek Thai cat, Trim had an overdeveloped personality

and a very loud voice. Olympia had bought her as a birthday gift to herself from a Buddhist monastery. After being blessed by a monk, she was smuggled aboard. It was a good life for a cat, lurking on deck, catching flying fish, and sleeping in the warm sun. She had to be hidden when the owner was there, which fortunately was only two to three weeks at a time. This proved to be no small feat when Trim was in season as she wandered forlornly around the ship bellowing *NOW! NOW! NOW!* Sometimes Dylan, who was not needed with the owner aboard, took Trim ashore, walking her on a leash, "trolling for girls" on the beach.[3]

Trim and Vargas got along well and shared a basket on the porch table. Cobber was sanguine about the whole cat business, his social status unassailable.

Dylan arrived not long after Trim, wearing a Yemeni turban and brimming with tales of adventure. He had a new passion, sailing.

He had only been with us a week when an email arrived from the ship's engineer, offering him a twelve-metre sailboat made of kauri, a prized New Zealand softwood. All he had to do was go get it. Problem was, it currently sat at the bottom of a harbour in

The Eby Rock marker at ebb tide.

Grenada, having sunk at its mooring during September's Hurricane Ivan. Dyl researched sailboat salvage and decided to give it a go, if only because not going would have meant never knowing what he'd missed. Bea was having kittens about this; there was looting in Grenada, and a curfew. Ninety percent of buildings had been damaged, including the jail.

TUESDAY, NOVEMBER 2

at 2:00 AM, a 6.6 earthquake strikes fifty kilometres off Tofino. We sleep through it.

WE HEARD about it, and the accompanying tsunami warning, the next morning on the radio. It was sobering to think we could have been washed away in the night. Down on the beach, there was no sign of anything unusual, which we put down to the low tide when the quake struck. It did prompt us to start searching for the storm shelter Mel had mentioned. All we had to go on was a wave of his arm and "back there on high ground where the trees are small." Jane, Mel had explained, had had a fear of trees crashing onto the beach house in windstorms.

We thrashed about unsuccessfully all morning.

Winter storms come early to the West Coast. Almost as soon as the last clear days of September pass, the first sullen grey clouds and steely October seas roll in. The little house took them all on the nose, with rain drumming against the windows and pattering against the shakes.

One night, a fierce westerly struck. It bent the hemlock in front of the house to such an extent that a branch that had appeared far from the house began whacking the front windows and the VHF radio whip aerial. There was a real possibility something would break. Climbing a ladder with a chainsaw in such conditions was out of the question, so I grabbed the shotgun, a Spanish classic I had inherited from my stepfather, loaded it with buckshot, and then went out into the horizontal rain. Bea held the flashlight. After following the wild gyrations of the branch, I fired. Twice. The two-metre branch was still there, chipped but still whacking the window and threatening to destroy the aerial. I reloaded and fired again. The branch vanished. I didn't see it go but we found it next morning on the lawn at the back of the house.

This first winter storm also brought with it our first storm surge, the force that piles logs like pick-up sticks along the shoreline. We went down to the beach to watch and were surprised to see the sand perfectly flat. The sea had receded beyond the south headland while the flooding river had lost its sand channel completely and spread like glass. As we watched, a wave surged around the south rocks and started up the beach, chased by a larger wave riding on top of it and catching up, then another on top of that, then another until we had something resembling a tidal bore.

Two walls of water, angry and agitated, raced toward us, one along the rock wall, the other up the middle of the beach. They hooked around in a pincer movement and collided. Instantly, a zipper formed, explosive, racing back out to sea at high speed. I'd heard of kayakers being thrown out of their boats trying to cross a zipper. Now we had our very own beach zipper. All the while, the main wall of turbulence charged up the sand faster than a person could run.

I scrambled onto a big log for a better view. Bea took up a position partway up the ramp. The wave reached the first logs to my left and they began to move, slowly at first, then faster. Water swirled past where I stood, rushing along the shoreline at the end of the beach, bending the overhanging alder and bouncing off rocks. The log I had been standing on started to float. Concerned I was about to be enveloped in another pincer movement, I leapt shoreward to another log, then to the ramp.

The remainder of the morning we spent watching the show from the porch, sipping tea.

Brabant Channel, between us and the Shot Islets, had a different but related act. Huge Pacific swells marched relentlessly past Bartlett toward Whitesands Beach on Flores. As they felt bottom in the shallow channel, their tops curled and crumpled, and spray slid down their backs like smoke. Gulls wheeled and dived.

As the tide reached its maximum, beach logs pushed high against the forest. An almost intact alder was having its branches ground off between two large jostling logs. The entire log-jam seethed each time a new surge swept in. A log fetched up on the sand and another was immediately thrust up and over it. There it hung like a teeter-totter.

When the tide receded, we walked the smoothly swept beach. Shivers of wind ran across the wet surface and ruffled the feathers of huddled gulls. They watched uneasily, assessing the risk of staying versus taking to the sky again. The storm front passed: clouds torn ragged as bright sky pushed through.

Fright and flight.

Tofino wave monkeys.

opposite Mel's beach, with a nice log come ashore.

Halfway along the beach, behind a small mountain of kelp, the surge had eroded some of the raised sandy camping bench popular with kayakers, revealing logs black from being buried for decades by drifting sand. Several new firewood alder had arrived, complete with crown and root system. There was also a beautiful new Sitka spruce log. Sitka spruce thrived in this area, with old-growth stands still present on Flores. A strong, light wood used since time immemorial by Indigenous Peoples also yielded the wing spars for Britain's Mosquito night-fighter bomber in the Second World War.

Wind and surf didn't keep all visitors at bay. When conditions were just right for them, the hotshot wave monkeys from Tofino would appear off our beach, sitting on their boards waiting for the first big sets to arrive, their boats anchored nearby. When specialized apps for surfers flagged six-metre southerly swells with a period around fourteen seconds, it meant some of the sweetest waves would be breaking on our beach and sandbar. With a

westerly or northwesterly swell, the surfers would be at Little Baja or Dunes, and the surf at our beach would be messy and chaotic.

We had our own knowledge and skills to build and refine, the quicker the better. To get to town, we had to figure out the best way to launch and land our inflatable in surf when it couldn't be avoided. Unlike a kayak, where arguably the most challenging part is getting *in* through surf, our boat was fast enough to stay between breaking waves. Indeed, by staying close to the back of a breaker it was possible to land on our sandy surf beach on any size of wave (dumping shore breaks on steep-to beaches would be another matter). Leaving the beach, however, usually gave the advantage to the kayak since its spear shape means it can more easily punch through and get beyond breaks that would backflip a small inflatable.

Big waves travel faster than a sea kayak, so when approaching the beach, the kayaker is constantly passed by fast moving waves and needs to resort to strategies such as bracing and sliding side-ways, or well-timed backpaddling to reach the beach and still be inside the boat.

As with a kayak, timing proved crucial when breaking out with the inflatable. It called for waiting in the soup till the largest waves in the set had passed, then going for the "soft spot." This can be tricky since soup usually indicates shallow water and a boat quickly turns on its skeg as the motor touches sand. Then the whole process has to start over.

Our motor being a four-stroke, it needed warming up before it ran reliably. As a "pull-start," it could take its own sweet time to restart after a stall. The first time I discovered this, I had every-thing lined up. The gap in the breakers appeared as I was inching closer to the impact zone. I called up the hare. The hare sprang to life. The boat jumped into the gap and the hare coughed, splut-tered, and quit. Frantically, I pulled the starter cord. Once, twice, three times. The boat turned side-on to the next breaking wave, which filled it with water and brought us close to capsizing. We wallowed back to the beach. I was grateful for the lateral buoyancy.

Lesson learned. From then on, when surf was likely to be an issue, Bea, dressed in her dry suit, would stand waist deep, back to the spent waves, holding the bow while I warmed up the motor. When a gap appeared and the motor was ready, I would yell. She would move clear, or climb into the boat if she was coming with me, then I'd toss the hare a carrot and we'd zoom out before the next breaker. At least, that was the theory.

On one occasion, when the surf was looking particularly gnarly, Bea was doing her job at the bow and taking sizable waves on her back. A big one came through. I saw it coming and tried to warn her, but there was not much she could do. She tensed. It exploded against her shoulders and she vanished beneath the boat, reap-pearing sputtering beside the motor. At least the prop hadn't been turning, and she still had her glasses on.

ROUTINES DEVELOPED as the season advanced. At first we had no access to email, so each week, weather permitting, I took a loaded memory stick to the Internet café in Tofino and returned with the contents of our inbox. It was how we stayed in touch with family and friends. While there, I would see to laundry and groceries. Bea had little interest in Tofino business and mostly stayed home, sometimes for weeks at a time—amazing for someone who'd had a people job.

Muddy boots triggered one of Bea's ongoing projects. During the morning walks she made a habit of collecting large butter clam shells. Before dropping them in her pocket, she tested each one for strength by standing on it, keeping only the thickest. Back at the house she'd fill each shell with sand and set them, round side up, in clusters as stepping-stones on the path to the back door. They were kind on bare feet and, at night, easy to see.

With people coming for Christmas, Bea's list of projects grew longer. She rummaged through her box of Sally-Ann offcuts and replaced the faded, ripped orange fabric on the living room bunk couches with sturdy, plum-coloured twill. She hand-sewed silk covers, fitted to hoops made from recycled garden hose, to keep mosquitoes and stray leaves from the water barrels, including the one inside the vestibule, now gathering rainwater from a clean part of the roof.

Meanwhile, I built window seats in the sunroom. They had lift-up lids and cavernous interiors where we stored enough food in metal tins to survive the apocalypse and then some. A foam cushion wrapped in a blanket served as a comfortable reading spot with a view of the corduroy ramp, and a couple of cedar bookshelves on the nearest wall meant you didn't have to stretch too far for the next book.

High on our priority list was building guest accommodation to lure our kids to visit and provide for friends. We marked out an area at the end of the workshop, cleared it of old lumber, and set some yellow cedar blocks into the ground for foundations. Each morning we walked the beach, checking out what had washed ashore and looking among beach logs for construction material. By examining the techniques used by Dick in the construction of the house, I was able to roughly copy the style and pick up a few tricks.

An obliging cedar came ashore in front of the house, providing blocks for shakes to cover the outside of the extension. A spruce log near the stream would provide for the inside walls.

We squared the spruce then fitted an Alaska mill to a hefty chainsaw and set about cutting clear, sixty-centimetre-wide planks.

It took two of us to operate the beast. I wrestled with the motor while Bea gripped the handle at the other end, easing the huge blade along. It was a noisy, slow job that covered both of us with fine white dust since the cut was along the grain. Cobber did not like the noise and though for a while he lay in the sawdust, he eventually got up, shook himself off, and wandered into the forest.

We never saw him again.

We searched for days, calling and whistling. Wolf tracks were everywhere, suggesting a new pack had arrived. We saw no sign of our old friend. Twelve years is a long friendship. On the mountain, Cobber had made friends with Sam, the wolf-dog next door. He had danced around intruding black bears till they bolted and had run for his life before a pack of coyotes. On a hiking trip to Mount Edziza, he had answered every prairie-dog whistle thinking it was mine. In the hills of Tuscany, he had been driven crazy by cuckoos, and in Madrid, lost in the park, had managed to find his way home alone across busy through-roads. And now, old and tired, and perhaps too curious, he had joined the wolves for good.

If I'd seen a wolf that first week, I'd have wanted it dead. But my urge for vengeance faded quickly, replaced by a sense of life unfolding as it should. Wolves eat domestic animals, particularly males, which are commonly lured by a female then killed by the rest of the pack. Female dogs, they say, are less vulnerable in this way, but I figured it was more about how hungry the wolf was.

"Better to die that way than be hit by a car in Vancouver," Dylan emailed philosophically when he read the sad news. Cobber had been his companion for half his life.

Still, hazing seemed a good idea over the winter months, something I had discussed with Francis, the park ranger we'd got to know over the summer. I happened to have the right rifle for the job—a surprising gift from our pacifist friend Deakins, who'd owned it forever but never used it: a fine Finnish-made .308. Although I hadn't shot much of anything in the previous thirty years, I had the permit and the skill, having worked as a professional deer shooter in my university days in New Zealand, where deer, imported without natural predators, were officially classified as noxious animals. They had destroyed much of the country's natural flora in partnership with rabbits and possums.

One evening, Bea and I were burning cut scrub on the beach. The sun was a ball of red through gently drifting smoke when

Cutting planks for our guest cabin project.

Amadeus appeared, trotting along the beach not a stone's throw from our bonfire. I bolted for the house and grabbed the rifle. The wolf, meanwhile, did not alter pace. It was just about to cross the stream when I pulled it into the crosshairs. I moved the sights in front of the animal to the orange reflection and fired. A geyser of water erupted two metres into the air right in front of the wolf's nose. It did a credible Disney imitation of air walking and took off streaking across the beach into the forest. Twice more we saw the wolf and twice more I fired close enough to remind it that being around humans can be hazardous.

"Wolves that are scared of people don't bite people," Francis had said.

Dylan came back at the end of a month with the carved name-plate of his boat, *Gesture*, the only part worth retrieving. It had been submerged too long. Despite the disappointment, he had grand tales of adventure salvaging other people's boats and bidding on a distress sale.

Les had ten months leave from the ship he was on, and he and Olympia would be heading to Australia together in the new year to cruise the Gold Coast on his private sailboat. Dylan had been dive master in charge of a twelve-metre turbo-diesel inflatable on the ship, so it seemed appropriate he should be the one to pick up Les from Tofino.

Apricot light played on surf and caught the snowy peaks as he brought in the little boat. Les arrived wearing one of the dry suits from the kayak videos, a change from his usual Hawaiian shirt, shorts, and flip-flops. He looked around and chuckled. He'd have expected no less from the lot of us. Trim purred loudly and rubbed against him in greeting.

Last to arrive for Christmas was Dawson, who surfed in by kayak a few days later. Dawson was a bold, wiry little Yorkshire-man, a climber, kayaker, caver, and teacher. I had met him when we first came to BC in 1978—he had been my boss as program director at Keremeos Outward Bound School and a friend ever since. An engineer as well as a film-making adventurer, he had built himself a live-aboard, twenty-metre steel sailboat, and had designed the kayak testing program for our magazine. In recent years, he had succeeded me on the board of trustees for the National Outdoor Leadership School, a Wyoming-based international outdoor school that ran a program in BC, and whose teachers sometimes turned up on our beach.[4]

Les and Olympia moved into Mel's guest cabin. Les was uneasy about cougars, so we presented him with a baseball cap with large eyes painted on the back. They only attacked from behind, we told him, dropping out of a tree on to your head. It was payback for the time he had let his crew (our kids) wander Komodo Island in flip-flops to look for dragons, those dinosaurs with poison teeth and a taste for tourists.

First night in their cabin, they awoke in the early hours. Some creature was outside. *Phwoosh. Phwoosh.* For the longest time they lay still, listening. When eventually they boldly looked out the window, there was a winter wren tossing leaves aside in search of bugs.

Christmas excess meant more rum than usual and a bottle of wine always open. On Christmas Eve, there were candles on the table. Bea took on all the cooking that day with the rest of us under her command. There was her famous tourtière, fresh crab, and smoked salmon, as well as mince tarts, shortbread, and the family Christmas cake from a recipe passed down from a great-great-grandmother on the Scottish border. To cook this cake just right in a wood stove was a labour of love and science combined.

Following Quebec tradition, we opened parcels and Christmas mail in the evening. It included a handwritten letter from Glenn, our Kiwi house-sitter.

Sitting here in my house in the Pohnpei rainforest at 3:30 AM, he wrote. *Wide awake for some reason. A power outage right now and a heavy rainstorm. So here I am writing from a forest, with rain, with candlelight. Apart from the temperature, seems like my island has a lot in common with your island.*

He had sent intricate woven-reed and shell ornaments for our Christmas tree. He was off to the Marshall Islands next.

Dawson had brought gifts carefully selected and wrapped by his sister Deanna, who was then also Deakins's sweetheart. More glue connecting the Johns.

Although this year there were just two of us, past Christmases we'd had up to five Johns around the table—four honorary uncles to the kids: Deakins, Dawson, Knight, and Carlton.

Knightly John, a geologist and master of jest, had sent a present from Smithers, where he now lived. It was in his best tradition:

Beach workout after
a crabbing run.

Strathcona watershed, Christmas.

typed up, elaborate instructions for an E-Z Home Computer of his own design. "You will have hours of fun putting it together, trying to make it work and vacuuming the carpet for the small bits you lost." His previous gift had been a folded cardboard kayak kit, accompanied by the dreadful Sally-Ann woven rug of a vulture we had traded back and forth over the years. Two of his presents to the kids, however, had become family treasure: a large ammonite and a jeweller's loupe.

The fourth uncle, our Aussie shipwright friend Carlton John, would be visiting us before long, he said. Dylan had been in touch with him over sailboat salvaging and buying tips.

For this first Christmas Eve on Vargas, there was flamenco guitar, Dyl's passion from an earlier time. Christmas Day saw more feasting, with turkey stuffed with chanterelles, a steamed pudding, then walks and naps.

On Boxing Day, it all came crashing down: a 9.1 earthquake off Sumatra had set off a wave of destruction around the Indian Ocean.

Phi Phi, an island community Les's ship often based at in Thailand, had been hit hard. Les had many good friends there. He took his phone to the point, one of a few places we had sporadic cell reception, and stayed there most of the morning. None of his friends responded, at least initially. Much coastline had been washed away, with damage all the way to Sri Lanka and South Africa. The tsunami had wrapped right around Madagascar. The dread was palpable, mounting with every news report.

The appalling tragedy gave us pause about our own vulnerability, given our exposed location so near the Cascadia subduction zone and our knowledge that tsunamis could also come from afar.

With 230,000 victims, the Sumatra Earthquake had been by far the deadliest in recorded history, as well as the third in magnitude.

Tsunamis generated by the strongest two in magnitude, a 9.5 and a 9.2, had reached Vancouver Island shores. The first, Chile's Valdivia Earthquake, had struck in 1960, followed four years later by the Good Friday South Alaska Earthquake. (Respective death tolls: 5,700 and 130.) Maximum wave height recorded at Tofino from each event was just over a metre for the first, just under two and a half metres for the second.

The Alaska event (March 27, 1964, 5:36 PM) brought particular chaos to the Hesquiaht First Nation settlement at the head of

Hot Springs Cove, where it hit five and a half hours later. Of the eighteen houses there, only two were spared; one floated away under the full moon. No lives were lost, although there *was* some swimming. The community relocated to higher ground farther up the inlet. Port Alberni was the most affected on this coast, owing to a magnifying funnel effect as the wave travelled forty kilometres up the Alberni Inlet: 55 houses washed away, 375 damaged, marinas and boats destroyed, and a seven-metre wave height for the record books.

As most British Columbians know, the risk posed by the subduction zone just off our shores has been estimated at a 30-percent possibility of a megathrust event (The Big One) occurring within the next fifty years. Major subduction earthquakes here are known to occur three hundred to five hundred years apart on average, and the last was pegged to 1700. It had an estimated 8.7 to 9.2 magnitude, and its tsunami reached Japan.

Motivated anew, we set off the next day in search of that emergency shelter. We looked for old blazes on stunted yellow cedar, pine, and yew. We bashed around for hours in a dwarf forest softened by rolls of deep moss that climbed the trunks. Old man's beard cascaded from the branches.

Dylan found the shelter on a plateau ten metres above the cabin. Not high enough to dodge a big tsunami wave, but better than staying below. He'd returned long after the rest of us had given up for the day, having blazed a trail home. The storm shelter turned out to be just a head-height shake hut with a rusted out tin stove beside a sleeping bench. Sphagnum moss and huckleberry bushes grew around it as well as the odd climbable tree. On the wall was a carved heart around the words DICK AND JANE.

Over more rum drinks, a candlelit debate ensued about what to do in case of an incoming tsunami. I favoured taking the inflatable out to sea. Bea said she was going to the shelter. All others stayed diplomatically neutral. Next day, we further opened the trail to the hut and marked it with reflective tape so we could find it by flashlight.

In addition, we set our battery radio to turn on at 0400 hours to catch any tsunami alerts. The reasoning was that if the Big One was local, it would shake us out of bed and we could make our move (or at least argue about it till the wave arrived). If it struck far away, say, Alaska, sometime after midnight, an 0400-hour announcement on the news would give us the time we needed. If the quake occurred after 0400 hours and we felt nothing, then it would be far enough away that we would hear about it before it arrived, in theory.

Behind the emergency shelter, we had noticed huckleberry bushes with old cut marks along a barely discernible hint of a trail heading south in the direction of high land near the centre of the island. Once the weather improved in the spring, we could find out if that trail led to an even safer refuge.[5]

Found it: the storm shelter.
MARLIN BAYES

Aftermath of a major storm surge.

3

DISCOVERIES

OLYMPIA AND LES LEFT for Australia, but not before taking both cats in to be spayed. Mercifully, the cries of *NOW! NOW! NOW!* came to an end.

Dylan too headed off, this time to England to visit a girlfriend, and we were left to our wind, our rain, and the cycle of tides.

One night, Bea awoke to an unusual noise. Without waking me, she put on her headlamp and went outside to investigate. Moments later, she called, "Come have a look at this! There's water halfway up the ramp!"

We stood and watched as a surge of water rushed out of the darkness and up the ramp, licking at our feet. As the surge retreated, we followed it down. Inside the boathouse, the inflatable had been afloat, pressed up against the kayaks hung from the ceiling. We pulled it out and winched it up the ramp to safety. The kayaks were fine so long as the boathouse itself did not float away and there seemed little chance of that given the size of the hawser attaching it to the tree, not to mention the parked tractor. In the morning, we discovered that massive logs had been rearranged in front of our entrance, indeed along the entire coast. Even Dan and Bonny's place, protected by islands off Tofino, was blocked off by logs.

We resumed work on the annex, our "Appendix Project." A slip of the tongue at the outset had given it the name we liked more. Some nice new spruce logs had been delivered by the storm as well as another cedar log someone had already started cutting into shake blocks and left bristling with wedges. Nothing was to

Making use of a good shake log.

code on the Appendix, of course, and because everything was based upon what came ashore, the four-by-four timbers of the frame were spruce, not fir.

At some stage, I think Jane had been planning a proper glasshouse because we found hundreds of fifty-centimetre glass squares wrapped in plastic stored in yet another shed that appeared out of the forest as more salal was pushed back. These would make fine windows.

Ibrahim and his long-suffering partner were doing their spring thing, with *glooks* and *clooks* as well as the usual *caw, caw*. They barrel rolled, tumbled, and dropped suddenly in their wild mating dance above the beach. Then it was just Ibrahim. Concerned, Bea looked up the bird book and learned that all was well and on time. The expectations were that by February they would have built their nest, in which Fatima would lay four to six eggs. Ibrahim would feed her during the three-week incubation. That pleased us. Once the chicks hatched, the parents would share feeding duties.

Mice sought refuge in the warmth of our home despite a high rate of attrition to cats and mousetraps. We made morning offerings of whacked or chewed mice on a slice of bread, and the ravens didn't mind if the heads were on or off. Sometimes we tried following Ibrahim when he took off with the food but their nest was well hidden and he was way too cunning to lead us to it.

Like Fatima, I was away for a time, to attend the Vancouver Boat Show that happens late January/early February each year. I had been there as a vendor of sea kayaks in the past, but this time I went in to work with Craig in my new capacity as a user of inflatables. It was a chance to renew old acquaintances and replenish the coffers. Bea assured me she was fine being alone for ten days.

"Besides," she said, "there's always the VHF for a real emergency."

By the end of March, work on the Appendix was complete. We put in the original, small wood stove from the kitchen and near it, in the corner, a sitting bench covered with a New Zealand sheepskin. Against the opposite wall we built a fold-down table and two bunks with driftwood sides. These were attached to a partition offering privacy to the next room and its double bed.

I put the glass to good use in a series of multi-paned windows and in the front door. Bea made curtains and we put Dylan's kauri *Gesture* dreamboat nameplate in a place of honour.

Honking their way north.

Our inaugural guests came for Easter—a family including our fairly new friend, the New Zealand consul, who had brought along a giant hamper of fine cheeses and wines. They had not known exactly what to expect, and the ride in the little inflatable likely did not reassure. Despite their posh diplomatic lifestyle, however, these were outdoor folk who fit right in on Vargas, including the kids—neither of whom complained about the outhouse or the tricky climb to the top bunk.

Spring gradually took hold and with it came the migratory birds. Flocks of western sandpipers dropped in on their way from Central America to their Arctic breeding grounds, scurrying back and forth in unison along the rolling edge of foam, feeding on creatures too small for us to see. More solitary stood the larger dunlins and the whimbrels, their curved beaks prodding the sand around piles of kelp for sandhoppers. High overhead, of course, great skeins of geese sped by in loose-ended squadrons, honking as they went.

In time, Dylan flew back from his adventures in Britain, but soon after reaching Vargas he became ill, struck with excruciating abdominal pain. Dawson was visiting at the time, so we left him in charge of the house while we rushed the boy to Tofino General Hospital. Our first evacuation. Diagnosis—kidney stone and blockage, likely the result of dehydration from operating a needle gun over the side of the ship in forty-degree temperatures. He was given serious painkillers and a reference to a urologist at the Port Alberni regional hospital. There, he was promptly popped onto an operating table and knocked out by a doctor named Mohamedali.

While he was still recovering on Vargas, we had a surprise visit from three teachers running an outdoor leadership course for their North Island College tourism class. One had been Dylan's kayak instructor when, as a teenager, he had briefly considered a future in guiding.

"Hell, Dad, there's no money in it," he'd said. He had a point.

That particular tourism program drew on Indigenous communities, and their guide courses ran early in the season, when weather conditions were less predictable. The "less predictable" showered heavy rains when they settled on our beach, so at our invitation the classes moved to stove-side in the Appendix. Bea got busy making hot chocolate and a batch of brownies. Our family accommodation had now proved itself as a practical beach refuge. The event marked the early opening of kayaker season.

AFTER THE long winter, our freezer was still well stocked with smoked salmon, but we fancied a change. My fabulous free-diving suit had been hiding away in a duffel bag. Each time I walked past, I thought I heard it give a little "Ahem!" so while Dylan was around, I decided to get back into it. We went to Mel's beach where the water behind the protective islet looked promising. With much grunting and wriggling, I managed to circumvent my damaged shoulder and get into the suit lubricated by enough liquid soap for a double load of laundry.

I entered the water, Hawaiian sling in hand, with Dyl riding alongside in a kayak to receive the piles of fish. Cold ached me to the bone between mask and hood. I loved free-diving but it had been mostly in warm places. This didn't feel like so much fun. The visibility was good—about ten metres—but the fish apparently mistook me for a clumsy sea lion. Even rockfish bolted and I never got close to anything. I had more success with the rock scallops so salvaged some dignity as a provider of gourmet seafood by collecting enough for a meal.

Getting out of the suit required the help of both Dylan and Bea. It might have been easier if they'd managed to stop laughing as one pulled and the other held while I did my best to prevent them taking my arm out at the shoulder.

In due course Dylan, his kidney all better, took off to join his friend D.J. working in film landscaping on a remake of *The Wicker Man* in Ladysmith. This resulted in an autographed photo of Nicolas Cage for the Appendix wall, a pickup truck we could borrow, and a new dog. A new dog? We were still mourning Cobber.

"You guys need a dog out here," Dylan insisted. "Besides, she is very sweet."

And she was, a friendly, mostly black, tricolour border collie "bitsa" (*bitsa* this, *bitsa* that). Born on a horse ranch in Alberta, she did not adapt well to her owner's move to East Vancouver, where she became an escape artist and was soon on her way to the SPCA. Dylan had just the alternative for her.

"Her name is Alida," he told us.

Bea shook her head.

"Nah. What do you think: Chiquita? Bonita . . . Lolita?"

Lolita it was, and we all received dog hugs and much body wagging as Lolita realized this was her new pack and her new name.

Then we did a really silly thing. Having decided that the best way to introduce her to Vargas the cat would be on neutral ground, we took Vargas out to the garden table then brought Lolita out to meet her. The cat took one look at the newcomer and bolted across the lawn, Lolita hard on her tail. Up the wall of the Appendix she flew to a ledge, ears back, hissing. Lolita thought it was a great game. They could play that again next time they met. As for Trim, she kept her cool and all was well.

Vargas Island was an easy fit for Lolita. There was no need to escape anywhere, and the beach offered a procession of feathered visitors to practice her herding instincts. We tried to break that habit when it came to migrating shorebirds, but the instinct was strong. Bonny chastised me when she saw Lolita doing the herding thing.

"When we had a dog, we kept it on leash at the beach," she said pointedly.

She was right, of course. Lolita would stop for a while upon command, but as soon as she figured no one was watching she was back at it, herding them away from much needed feeding. At least they could always drop over to Mel's beach for a restful meal.

Lolita disapproved of eagles ("squeaky, squeakies" as we called them) and as soon as she heard or saw one, she belted off down the ramp after it, even if it was high overhead. Interestingly, when the ospreys made their seasonal return, she accepted them, as she did the kingfisher operating from the edge of the lagoon.

Her relationship with ravens turned out to be more nuanced. Games were involved. She chased them away from their morning mouse and they tugged her tail when she was napping in the sun, just as they liked to do with wolves, apparently to test their reaction time.

Wolves. Lolita first encountered them days after she arrived. We were walking Dunes beach when a pack of four emerged from the forest two hundred metres away. The moment she saw them, she took off in their direction. I imagined a swift and bloody encounter. I whistled and yelled, but we had not yet established a currency of commands. She kept running toward them.

Raven teases dog,
dog chases raven.

"Down!" I roared.

To my surprise, she stopped in her tracks and lay down, staring intently at the wolves, who stood still, waiting for lunch to arrive.

ON APRIL 22, Earth Day, we discovered that Mel's island, accessible from the beach at low tide, was a mass of wildflowers. Nestled among sun-warmed rock were mossy pools lined with miniature irises and fly-catching sundews. Pushing through last year's dry grass, bouquets of flame-red paintbrush and black lilies grew in profusion. Coastal Indigenous communities, we had read, harvest the lily bulbs as a source of carbohydrates. Carefully, we dug up some for ourselves, their bulbs like fat grains of rice. We would transplant them near our house.

A riot of wild roses grew on the sunny side in the shelter of storm-dwarfed spruce. Nearby, a gnarled bleached log tossed high on the rocks by some ancient storm held posies of yellow monkey flowers in cracks that could hold moisture. Mats of flowering stonecrop mingled with wild strawberry, wild onion, and purple self-heal. There were orchids we had never seen before, together with several varieties of saxifrage wedged into cracks in the rock.

Inspired, we returned to our house garden, now planted with mail-order seed and soft-neck garlic. A newly built, slender garden box held neat rows of carrot tops we could admire from an attached bench seat. Truck rims we had found behind the workshop were repurposed as planters and seeded with perennial arugula. I nearly capsized the boat bringing in a monster load of steer manure from town.

Between high tides, we collected wheelbarrow loads of the kelp storms piled ashore, leaving it on high ground to compost and be rinsed by rain. Then, as the weather improved, we spread it and planted young corn and zucchini directly into the sand—our experimental beach garden. The seedlings thrived, watered diligently with buckets from the stream.

Mel arrived to check for winter damage to the tower, give his lawn its seasonal haircut, and see how we were doing.

"It's looking nice," he said glancing around, reassured.

Next, BC Parks's fancy twin-engine aluminum cabin cruiser turned up, anchoring in the shelter of Burgess. A ridiculously small rubber dinghy with Francis and a new sidekick headed for

Clockwise from top left: Earth Day on Mel's island; black lilies, paint-brush, and self-heal; sedum and wild strawberry; a monkey flower, so bold.

our beach, oars flailing fiercely against a current at least as strong as the oarsman. Aboard the mother ship, a third man watched the struggle through binoculars.

The pair carried their boat up the beach then set off, each equipped with a long-handled shovel and a backpack. I intercepted them mid-beach, on their way to dig a new toilet for beach campers.

"So how was the winter?" Francis asked, smiling.

"Comfortable," I said.

"What about wolves?" then, seeing Lolita, "I thought wolves killed your dog."

"Different dog. This is Lolita." Lolita came up and presented an ear for scratching.

"No problem with wolves," I said. "I hazed them a couple of times, and Lolita seems to get it. We often see tracks in the mornings."

"There is a pack of five around the Inn. They're habituated."

"I'll let you know what I see," I said.

He pulled out a business card and handed it to me.

"That's my direct cell number. Call any time you see a problem," he said.

I TRIED to visit my elderly mother each year and this was to be her ninety-fifth birthday, so in early May I headed into Tofino, parked my kayak at Dorothy's boat rack, and flew to New Zealand.

The old lady still walked an hour each day and managed her own affairs. She had a new laptop and an ongoing battle with the digital world. She moaned when I promised to reply immediately to any email I received.

"It's good for you," I said. "Keeps your mind sharp."

Bea, meantime, was dealing with the first campers on the beach since the tourism group. The Vanier school party arrived for their annual visit and immediately dropped by the house. Lolita was a huge hit with the kids but kept stealing their Frisbee and running into the sea with it when she became too hot from trying to run it down.

Even without large projects there was much for Bea to do—the gardens to tend to and pieces to be collected for sculptures she was working on. She tried fishing but was a bit early for the bluebacks.

Timeless rainforest on the way to the summit.

"So how was it?" I asked when I got back. "Did you get lonely?"

"It was great," she said. "You should do that more often."

Time soon came to explore the path toward high land we'd noticed behind the emergency shelter. The trick was to find the huckleberry bushes with old cut marks, then cut back the encroaching vegetation after scrambling across steep gullies and streams, through dense wetlands jammed with salmonberry and devil's club. The clues were twenty years old, a cut branch here and an overgrown blaze there. Blowdowns across the trail needed the chainsaw. Eventually we came out into a wide clearing of sphagnum moss with silver spires of drowned swamp cedar before the final ascent of a forested slope.

The last kilometre was a steep scramble, handhold to handhold beneath a canopy of hemlock and fir, through heavy fern and moss still dripping from a shower during the night. We pushed through the last scrubby trees to a rounded dome of lichen- and moss-covered rock. A white plastic bucket for rainwater reminded us we were not the first to that summit.

No sooner had we arrived than Ibrahim swooped down to see what we were doing. To the west, north, and south, forested islands lay scattered in a calm blue ocean; calm, that is, until you looked more closely and saw swells licking white against black

Dappled magic.

rock. The offshore fogbank clung to the horizon. Behind us, the mountains of Strathcona had a fresh dusting of snow.

On the way home we collected wild violets from a mossy streambed to place around the pond we planned. We timed the walk—forty-five minutes.

There was still much to explore. When Alain, a wildlife photographer and longtime friend, visited from France, it was an excuse to go find Monks Lake. It appeared as a small tarn on the satellite photo, with a stream running out to the south end of Little Baja. The stream being too well hidden, we set off crashing and thrashing through thick forest on an easterly compass bearing. Then, quite suddenly, we were back eighty million years.

We stood, stared, and soaked in the abrupt silence.

"It just needs a lily-munching dinosaur," Bea whispered. She was mud-spattered and scratched, a marooned time traveller.

"Maybe a moose," Alain ventured.

"Sorry, Alain. No 'meese' on Vancouver Island."

Waist-high cattails grew on soggy land between huckleberry bushes at the edge of the forest, and a fringe of lily pads bursting with yellow extended far out into calm water.

Once there, we didn't quite know what to do next, so while Bea and Alain started on their sandwiches, I waded out onto the gnarled roots and cut some rhizomes to stock the pond.

Watching Alain spend hours setting up a picture of monkey flowers on a log or starfish in a tidal pool got us thinking about getting out our cameras again. Fortunately, we still had all my professional 35mm cameras and lenses. So, when a rare stranding of millions of turquoise by-the-wind sailors occurred, Bea and Alain were out there for hours getting closeups of the iridescent jellyfish before they died, dried, and lost their sheen.

OUR FRIEND Kenchenten (another John, another Brit) was our partner in the sea kayak videos, but also very much involved in films about cooking. So, when he came to visit, we stood back.

"So, what have we got?" he said, rotund and bewhiskered, sniffing around the kitchen cheerfully.

We took him to a chanterelle patch and picked a basket load along with some oyster mushrooms growing on a mossy alder log. On the way back to the house, he added a couple of young bolete

Lookie, lookie: Chanterelles, gooseneck barnacles, mussels!

JUNE 15, 7:50 PM. A 7.2 magnitude earthquake hits off the northern coast of California. A tsunami warning is issued for the entire West Coast including Tofino. The warning is withdrawn an hour later.

mushrooms, then he cruised our herb garden, snipping chives, dill, parsley, sage, rosemary, and oregano.

"Ooh, I do love these wood stoves," he said, rubbing his hands together over the warmth of the hotplates. "And this one is a beauty, the heat so smooth and even. How about we make some focaccia?"

And as we watched, he massaged flour in a bowl with bubbling yeast and created a giant rubbery slug in a warm, flour-dusted iron pan.

"And these warming ovens... great inventions. Should have them on all modern stoves. There. It will be ready for baking by the time we get back with mussels."

Down to the rocks, where Kenchenten walked the shoreline, carefully picking mussels for size and quality.

"Lookie, lookie," he cried, excitedly pointing to a cluster of what looked like withered grey fingers with deformed nails. "Gooseneck barnacles. These little beauties sell for over a hundred dollars a kilo in Italy."

Carefully, he slipped a knife along the base and removed a small number.

"Just take what we need," he said. "Keeps the rest fresh."

On the way back he added some clean whips of bull kelp.

"Perfect for pickling." He sniffed it affectionately.

Back at the house, he rolled the herbs into the now puffed-up dough and painted it with olive oil, dusting it with rock salt and

Dawson doing his thing.

opposite Sea fog moves in on Burgess Islet. "Antidune" sand patterns usually indicate the best spot to land a kayak.

oregano. The house smelled like Italy. He made a cream sauce and dropped in the steamed, shucked mussels and carefully peeled barnacles, grating in zest of lemon, and tossing in chopped garlic, parsley, and a cup of Parmesan. Fettuccini, boiled, strained, and sprinkled with olive oil had the simmering sauce added at the last moment. The mushrooms had been fried with onion as a side dish, and a bowl of freshly picked lettuce Bea had garnished with daylilies and nasturtium sat dressed in the middle of the table.

"Timing is of the essence," Kenchenten announced triumphantly as everything came together at once. We sat at the table with a glass of a particularly nice red he just happened to have in his backpack and broke the hot bread with our fingers.

His focaccia, bannock, and candied bull kelp became Vargas specialties.

The kayak video project was coming to an end. We had completed our *Getting Started*, *Navigation*, and *Weather* videos, and Dawson had footage "in the can" for the next in the series, *Oceanography*. To finish, he needed an in-your-face shot of a boomer. A boomer happens when the largest of a set of waves passes over a normally submerged rock and the trough exposes its top. The wave then steepens and crashes. *Boom!*

We located a convenient example half a mile off Ahous Bay, south of Blunden Island. I nosed the inflatable in from the downside of the break while Dawson crouched at the bow with a waterproof camera.

"Closer!" he yelled.

I turned and took another run. This was not the sort of place anyone would normally take a boat. Dawson, in his yellow dry suit, only saw the image on the screen.

"Closer," he said. "We need to get in closer."

"Okay, okay," I grumbled, manoeuvring the inflatable till we were almost on the rock. A big wave obliged, curled over, smashed down onto the boat, half-filled it, then spat us out. Dawson floundered afloat in the middle of the boat, clutching his camera.

"Dammit," he said, "the camera wasn't running."

"Dammit" was about the worst cuss word Dawson used.

I hit the throttle. The water inside the boat sloshed over the transom in one huge rush and we were away.

"That's it," I said. "Time to pull the plug."[1]

AUGUST ARRIVED and our top garden was a riot of carrots, cauliflower, and beans. There was ongoing guerrilla warfare with slugs and some bugs that invaded the cauliflower, but overall we declared the venture a success.

Meanwhile, the beach garden had disappointed. With the arrival of hot northwesterlies, sand flew with the wind, snaking across the sun-baked flats, forming little dunes that built inexorably around our garden and the log rounds we had set up as a barrier. Drifting sand found gaps and spilled through, forming little deltas that covered the young plants. Gradually, sand covered the rounds themselves. It was an unforeseen force of nature. After one particularly prolonged blow, all we could see of our garden were disrupted patterns of drifting sand. Next year we'd try something different.

Sea fog was another force we had to learn to live with, of course. The problem was made especially plain the day I was at the north rocks casting into the fog, when a sport fishing boat appeared out of the whiteness and someone called, "Which island is this?"

Local flyers had their own ways of coping, I found out shortly thereafter. Fishing at that same spot, I heard an aircraft engine in fog so dense the tower on Eby was barely visible. As the sound grew louder, I started involuntarily backing away—it seemed to be coming straight for me. Suddenly a floatplane blasted out of the mist, skimming the water, flying below the level of the tower. The face of the pilot registered, almost level with where I stood. With a roar the plane passed and vanished following the shoreline. I listened to the sound fading into the distance, preparing myself for a crash that never came. What would happen if it met a vessel with a high mast, I wondered.

Sometime that summer, an old friend and her teenaged son came to visit, a birthday trip for him. Fog had socked us in for days, but young Nick was keen to get out in the boat fishing. We took a bearing for Blunden Island and then located one of my favourite fishing spots near what we'd come to know as "Big Boomer" or "BB Rock" for short. That ugly dome of barnacle- and kelp-encrusted rock boomed at anything below half tide and occasionally during the largest swells when the tide was higher.

Visibility hovered around fifty feet. I dropped anchor a safe distance from BB Rock and turned off the motor. The tide was rising and the explosions in the fog grew less frequent. We dropped our lines to the bottom and soon had a load of rockfish. I was on edge, being so close to a clear and present danger when, out of the corner of my eye, I glimpsed an unusual wave break over barnacles, within arms reach of the boat. The anchor's dragged, I thought, my nerves screaming. I felt dizzy—the land seemed to be moving. I braced for the fold-over break, only to see a large unblinking eye checking us out from the front of the land mass. A huge humpback whale swished by and sank beneath the waves.

"Wow! Wowie! Holy shit!" Nick exploded.

A boat-watching whale; nice reversal.

"I think we have enough fish for today," I said, winding in my line. Then, just like that, the fog lifted and the world looked bright and normal again.

By the time we got back, a wild, hairy young man had pulled his homemade wooden kayak up in front of our place.

"Oh man, have you got any dope?" was the first thing he said. "I had no idea that stuff was addictive. I ran out two weeks ago. Man, I need a joint."

I forget his name, but he was from Alberta and had built the five-metre kayak without ever having paddled one. Fortunately, he chose a good design, and he did a nice job, inlaying the deck with symmetrical patterns of contrasting wood and coating it in epoxy inside and out for strength. When it was finished, he asked someone in a kayak shop what else he needed and was sold a load of gear. So far, so lucky. Then he asked the sales gal where she would go kayaking if she had the summer off.

"I'd paddle down from Alaska to Vancouver," she said.

So this guy, who'd never been in a kayak, shipped his boat to Prince Rupert and set off paddling down the outside. He had to have been a fast learner because he chose the wildest, most exposed route possible.

"Fish, fish, fish. I'm sick of fucking fish. I've had fish every day for the last month. And then I ran out of dope!"

"Ha, we just caught some rockfish and I was going to offer you some," I said.

"Anything but," he groaned.

We found a decent steak in the freezer and that pleased him. Then we went to chat to some kayakers from Bellingham who'd arrived that afternoon. I offered them some fish, still so fresh they twitched. They were about to prepare supper and were delighted at the prospect, but their faces dropped when they realized the fish were whole. None of them knew what to do with a whole fish. Meanwhile, the Albertan was drooling at the sight of their packaged ravioli. He told his story and made a deal. He would fillet the fish in exchange for ravioli. The Americans showered him with packets of processed food and he kept them regaled with stories while he filleted and deboned the catch.

Next day, he moved on to Tofino, where he could find plenty of what he craved. A month later, we received a letter: "Made it to Victoria no problem."

By the end of summer we'd made friends with many strangers, and Lolita the same. She had in fact become the visitors' darling and

She *could* be mistaken for a wolf.

Sea otter in repose.

achieved an online presence. She would greet each new party as they arrived, taking it upon herself to protect these oddly dressed people in their flimsy cloth houses, especially if they had kids. She'd lie outside their tents and bark when wolves, real or imagined, came too close. I would frequently have to go fetch her in the evenings and explain that, no, she was not a neglected lost dog. If she could, of course, she would sneak back to resume her guard duty.

Though there to protect, Lolita was at times mistaken for a wolf. In one story reported to us, a woman who did not realize Lolita was there got up for a midnight pee, well primed with stories of wolves attacking kayakers. From the shadows emerged the loving Lolita. The woman's screams woke the entire beach and brought everyone out of their tents. In another story, which we were there to witness, Lolita ran to greet a couple carrying gear from a kayak at low tide. Seeing what appeared to be a black wolf charging from the forest, they dropped their bags and bolted for their boat. We had to go talk to them.

Lolita had a special bark when wolves really were around. There was a shrill edge to it that got your attention. She was also way too brave for her own good, perhaps counting on her human pack, and so we worried. At least she had a good top speed, unlike Cobber, who in old age had been down to a fast trot.

Once when Bea and I were fishing off the south rocks at low tide, Lolita came running toward us, barking her wolf bark, wolf in hot pursuit. Seeing us, the wolf stopped with a look of disgust, turned and trotted away. *Not them again.*

Lolita was also learning when not to run. Later that day, at the same spot, she found a wounded sea otter resting on the rocks and lay beside it very quietly till it swam away toward Flores. We watched with her until we could no longer see the dark round head in the distance. The sea otters' miraculous comeback had not pleased everyone, that much was clear. Some local crab and sea urchin fishers saw them as competition and shot them when they thought no one was watching.

With the approach of fall, the crowds of campers started thinning again. Ibrahim and Fatima drove their chicks off the beach. It was sad to watch the young ravens fluffing their neck feathers, heads lowered, begging for food. Instead, they were pecked and knocked over; confused and upset, they would return, pleading, only to be knocked down again. Eventually they retreated and

top Nail lichen, also known as devil's matchstick.

bottom Dry mossy summit.

sat in a tree a hundred yards from the house. There they were dive bombed by their mother and father. It was brutal. One morning, they had gone—doubtless off to join a gang of similarly disaffected youth.

By then, the southbound migration of young birds was in full swing and the first squadrons of geese honked gently by. Lolita was introduced to the leash—at least when Bonny was there.

A blooming of chanterelles had just occurred thanks to sea fog condensation so I was out mushroom picking behind the main campsite the day Dan and Bonny landed with a new group.

Dan was explaining basic routine for privacy using the bush toilet.

"Just hang the rope across the path, and that will be the signal that the toilet is occupied. Nobody will disturb you," he said.

That was when I emerged with my basket of mushrooms, wearing my Robin Hood-style, knee-length woollen bush jacket from New Zealand, with moss and twigs stuck to it.

I said hi to the assembled group and left Dan to explain.

During the summer, Glenn, a paddler from Chilliwack, had dropped by and looked critically at our garlic crop. We felt proud of our ripening plants, but no: "It's not a good variety," he said. "No flavour. I'll send you some Russian Red."

We thought nothing more of it till a shoebox full of plump purplish cloves arrived in the post, with instructions to plant in October.

The planting of the garlic marked the end of one cycle and the beginning of another. It had been a full year since we had moved in and we had the sense we were just glimpsing the complexities of life on the beach. Cycles existed within cycles and we were just nudging in.

DYLAN BOUGHT himself a long board. Since he had surf right on the doorstep of his second home, it seemed silly not to have one. Lolita, however, considered surfing highly irregular and would wait at the water's edge anxiously till Dyl came ashore shivering and tired. One day, we heard frantic barking; there was Dyl catching a wave and right beside him, a gray whale. He almost surfed onto its back and never saw it. That confirmed all of Lolita's worst fears.

As the last gray whales headed south, Olympia came back from Australia. She had her tropical golden locks and bright blue eyes again, as well as a small black and white terrier named Bungie. Bungie had been labelled a Jack Russell when purchased as a puppy from a Surfers Paradise pet store, but the ears kept growing till they resembled those of a large fruit bat.

"Ugly," Bea declared, "but endearing."

Les, meanwhile, had returned to his job skippering the billionaire's yacht and sold his sailboat, marking the end of an era.

Olympia quickly found work in Tofino as a live-in nanny for local doctors Pam and John and their three children. Bungie moved in with them. At the local doggy park, it was discovered that Bungie could twist and dodge so fast no other dog could match her, a trait that might serve her well on Vargas. Amazingly her ears could rotate 180 degrees to gain a sonic image of what was behind, be it bicycle or wolf. She quickly got the hang of detecting and chasing mink from under beach logs.

ONE OF Trim's favourite activities was to climb a tree to a point from which she could not return unaided. She was, it turned out, addicted to being rescued. Usually, she would climb several metres till she reached a comfortable spot and cry out loudly so one of us would be obliged to retrieve her, now purring.

I was about to head to Vancouver to catch a flight to Japan when she did it again. It was nighttime and she was high up a scrawny hemlock near the porch this time, sitting on the lowest branch, yowling. There was no way we could have climbed that tree and she was too high for the extension ladder. Something had to be done.

I measured the distance and rested the rifle against the corner of the workshop. Bea held the flashlight. I set the crosshairs on the limb where the cat lay with her nose five centimetres from the trunk. Gently, I squeezed the trigger. There was a humongous bang and a belch of flame. (It is spectacular to fire a .308 in the dark, I discovered.) The branch splintered and the cat leapt into the air, landing back on the now slightly drooping limb. The cut, however, was only partial and the cat had landed forward of her previous position, so her head was now directly above the splintered wood. Her meow had acquired a certain shrillness.

We noticed that each time she meowed she turned her head to one side, then with the next meow, to the other. With her head turned to meow on the far side, the partial cut would appear for a

Off to catch a flight to Japan.

couple of seconds, just clear of the side of her head. In a William Tell moment, I reloaded. *Bang*!

Down came the branch, cat hanging on. They landed safely in the salal. Trim was purring when we picked her up.

During the night, big swells arrived. Nasty, chaotic surf pounded the beach and westerly storm-force winds drew streaks of spume across the waves between us and Burgess Islet. The inflatable didn't look like a good bet and I still had that plane to catch.

I loaded my kayak. The "good clothes" and slides needed for my talk went into a waterproof bag and my briefcase into the sealed stern compartment.

Bea held the bow into the waves while I secured my spray-skirt and attempted to make sense of the chaos in front of me. A quick peck on the lips and I pushed off, holding into the soup as I searched for a gap. It appeared, and I was away, clawing at the water for speed.

As soon as I reached the break zone, a nasty side wave moved into the gap, curled over me, and crashed down, burying me. I was close to surfing backwards but managed to get going again, and by the time the next wave arrived, I was up to speed. This time the bow punched through the crest. The wave hammered me in the chest, but momentum stayed with me. Another big wave and I broke clear, picked up by the current of a flooding tide. In no time, I was around the corner and bombing along Calmus Passage in a following sea.

Free as a bird!

How Bea recollects my time away:

I SNAP PHOTOS AS you leave, but my hands are shaky. Am I recording your demise? I know you'll brace the instant you have to, because with that bum shoulder of yours you can't risk a capsize and roll. Now I can't see you anymore. Are you in the clear? Are you at Eby yet?

Japan is a place John is fond of, and I looked forward to the stories when he got back. Most of these will be about food and friends.

Dan was joining him on the flight, and would, I knew, practice his Japanese on him mercilessly all the way to Narita; they'd done this before. What time was their flight again? I might catch a glimpse of their plane from here—the flight path was right above me.

Takehiro would pick them up from the airport. This was the Take I know, the one who, as a nineteen-year-old, had come to our shop door saying, "I want learn kayak." And so he had. Dan had taken him under his wing and taught him well. The two eventually paddled around Vancouver Island together. The next time we saw Take was in Tokyo; he was on staff at the kayak store spawned there by ours. Since then, he'd established himself as an instructor, grown a family, and organized this latest trip—a training course to Ito Peninsula involving a large group.

Because there had been two translations of John's kayak manual and he was of a venerable age, he was regarded there as a teacher with a capital T, as was Dan, despite the lesser vintage. Which brought about such invitations.

Our friends—Take, Taka, Rollie the Tokyo Yukoner, Shinya-san the Master—I would soon hear how they all were, and salivate or recoil at John's food stories. One year, it had been live minnows artfully caught with chopsticks, dipped in hot-pepper soy sauce, and eaten alive. Thrilling.

"What'd you do while I was gone?" John would ask. I'd have made a list for him, knowing that as events fade in our memory they can also shape-shift like clouds on the wind, spoiling their reporting value.

Being on one's own for two or three weeks triggers a brain switch: you go from active/reactive to active/contemplative. You listen to the inner voice more, you switch to coffee in the morning because, really, what *is* it about Earl Grey tea? You talk to your animals about more serious things. And of course, you become more particular about the way things are arranged on windowsills. You beachcomb at greater leisure now and add to your collection of sea glass, moon snails, and jingle shells with fresh intent. You are, however, open to revelation about what to add to your collection. For instance, sea lion whiskers.

That particular November, a large sea lion carcass, still brown and fresh, washed up on the beach not far from the path to Mel's. Cause of death: a bullet hole through the neck. Not wanting to attract wolves and scavengers to our home beach by slicing the creature open for them, I made a plan to rope it up so that, dry-suited, I could yank it back out to sea on the receding tide.

While waiting for a tide high enough to float it for me (my attempt to move it down with a hand winch having failed), I started on a careful forensic photo session, which went from scientific enquiry to outright fascination. Freshness helping, I fell in love with a carcass. (I was not alone in this—Lolita shared my interest.) Particularly stirring were the creature's elongated, five-toed, gun-metal-grey hind flippers. They were blubbery, soft, and wrinkled like the skin of an old person. When the time came, I squeezed my study subject's fore flipper goodbye and pulled seaward as far out as I could wade. Then, sad but glad, I let go of the rope and away it went (minus the whiskers, which are still in my possession).

The weather had its vagaries. On days of hard rain, I took Vargas in and she stationed herself by my books and magazines at the front room table. (Of the two cats, she was the bookish one. She pawed at pages and lay on them. Trim was more into sun patches, laser pointer dots, and fish.)

I started on a new hardcover, *Chasing Clayoquot*. I browsed the stack of *New Scientist* back issues Deakins had dropped off for us.

Good company.

I caught up with the newspaper and magazine articles I had waiting from the subscriptions pile: the *Weekly Guardian* with the *Economist* for contrast, *Actualité* for a French-language fix.

I missed spoken French. Radio-Canada wasn't yet reaching here. But I had CDs and cassettes, and story recordings in my Vancouver cousin's voice.

Sometimes I sought the company of strangers close by and tuned in to the Ahousaht VHF channel. So-and-so had done baking to which her friends were welcome, so-and-so was on the ferry over, so-and-so expected a Co-op grocery order dropped off at First Street dock. (Useful knowledge, that. And the slight lilt, the pleasantly unhurried nature of the chatter itself made for good listening.)

Bungie was with me on a beach holiday. One day, the wolves came by, howling. The dogs went wild inside the house. The pack sat expectantly on the sand watching the front door. I took out the rifle, locked the dogs inside, and chambered a round.

John had pestered me to learn to use the darn thing, invoking the tale of the Alaska woman who'd watched a grizzly walk off with her toddler while she tried to figure out which cartridge to put in the gun.

Bang! I fired into the sand. The wolves scattered. Done.

Back inside, I was greeted by two very attentive dogs, particularly Bungie, who had a special aversion to firearms and probably figured that if she stayed close, the thing would not make that noise again. She was wrong. I ejected the spent shell case and confirmed our shared views about guns as I was putting it away by accidentally discharging it into the doorpost right beside our little Aussie. She bolted upstairs and hid for two hours. John had seemingly failed to point out, or perhaps I had failed to recall, that ejecting a shell rechambered the next. From that day onward I'd be sticking to bear bangers.

I wondered if John would notice the new hole.

Not long before his return, as if to herald it, a small, perfect Japanese glass ball materialized on our beach, floating in a puddle. Our first. It was not a dream.

In praise of buoyancy.

NEAR CHRISTMAS, Olympia and Bungie were already at the cabin with Bea and Dawson, and I went into Tofino to pick up Dylan and do last minute shopping. Dyl had brought an armload of gifts along with the frozen turkey.

"You'd better hurry," said Vince the wharfinger. "They are predicting forty-five-foot swells."

Swells that size would increase by a third when they felt bottom in Brabant Channel. What I didn't know was what that would feel like in a three-metre inflatable.

"Yep. We're on our way," I said, casting off with a pang of guilt—this was exciting.

A light westerly kicked up a chop as we sped along the north coast of Vargas. We could see waves exploding on Monks Rock and Catface already—the big swells had arrived.

At Eby Rock we got to appreciate the full effect. Gigantic breaking waves four hundred metres between crests swept the channel, spray smoking down their backs as they cruised along. We'd seen "smokers" from the safety of the beach; now we would get to feel them.

"Should we head back?" Dylan asked.

"Nope. We can make it," I said, standing up for a better view. We had less than eight hundred metres to go and if worse came to worst we could pull into the beach early. "We just need to get out a bit further so we can get between two waves."

Eby was completely washed down as we passed it. I'd never seen anything close to that before. My plan was to get out as far as we could then cut in between two waves, run parallel to the break, then hit the beach before the next wave. Unfortunately, an outflowing tide had kicked up side waves I had not noticed. They ran at right angles to the main waves with a violent, unpredictable action. As we turned to make our run, one "blew up" under our bow. The boat almost stood on its transom. The anchor and chain flew out of the bow locker and landed, along with the turkey and Christmas presents, between where Dylan and I sat clinging on to the handles on the tubes, staring at each other in disbelief. Dyl pulled a face.

"Yikes! Lucky that anchor didn't go over the side," he said with a nervous laugh.

I gave the motor full throttle.

To port, a mighty wave broke on its way to the beach. To starboard, another reared up, translucent like a wall of bent glass. It broke on the sand bar with a spectacular thump. We should have been doing twenty knots but the boat felt sluggish. We plowed through white swirling froth. I checked the throttle. The hare said we were going for it but it felt like we were dragging kelp. Then the penny dropped—with the water still aerated from the broken wave, the propeller was not getting its normal grip. I eased closer to the incoming breaker and got more traction. By the time that wave caught up, we had arrived at our landing approach. We swung toward the beach and pulled up the motor as it touched sand, letting the soup carry us sideways. We hadn't shipped a drop of water.

"That wasn't so smart, Dad," said Dylan.

"Unappreciative youth," I snorted.

Rain, rain, and more rain.

4

THE THREE DAUGHTERS
AND THE LONG DRY

FROM THE SOLSTICE UNTIL mid-January, there was an almighty deluge; pounding rain day after day after day. The sand became liquefied. The shell path flooded.

And yet this new year also held the opposite in store—a record, summer-long drought so bad it would lead to emergency water rationing in Tofino. (Vargas managed on its reserves.)

FEBRUARY. BOAT show month and I was off again, by kayak to avoid leaving the inflatable at the dock for a week. Walls of rain driven by a fierce southerly swept up Calmus Passage, with big wet snowflakes flying in the mix. Bungie had been staying with us and Olympia wanted her back. The poor little thing complained at having to leave the warmth of the stove, and stood, back arched, at the water's edge as I prepared to leave. I scooped her up and shoved her inside the kayak, where she promptly curled up on my lap, shivering.

The wind whipped up steep waves in Calmus, every one washing the boat down and slapping me in the chest. My bad shoulder started to grind, but there was no stopping or I would be going backwards. It took four hours without a pause to reach Tofino and there was water slopping about in the boat when I dragged it onto the beach. By then, I'd missed my bus and I cursed the choice we'd made to live without a vehicle.

"We don't need a car," we convinced each other. "We have a boat!"

Fatima in spring preening mode.

I'd have to hitchhike—not ideal for a greybeard. The rain drummed on the hull of the boat as I loaded it onto one of Dorothy's racks and clicked the padlock. Bungie stood immobile, hunched, ears folded down to keep out the rain. She wouldn't move so I carried her to Olympia's, then back I went, onto the road.

Hitchhiking was not new to me; I'd spent years hitching around South America, North Africa, and Asia, but I was in my twenties then. This felt decidedly weird. At least I had good raingear and a waterproof pack. The first vehicle to come along was a new pickup loaded with crates of live crab. It pulled over. The driver was Asian and introduced himself as Tan. His hands were like leather, his face hard and creased in the way of the sea. Suddenly a smile broke through.

"I recognize," he announced happily. "I see you in little boat."

I held my hands against the heater. I had good circulation, but today my hands were numb, white, and wet.

I took a chance.

"Are you from Vietnam?" I asked.

"I boat person," he said, suddenly serious. Nodding. "Escape Vietnam in little boat. Long time on sea. Many peoples die."

"I North Vietnam soldier," he added proudly, after a pause. "Kill many Americans. They bomb school, so we school in tunnel. My village catch American pilot. We kill him."

BOAT SHOW proceeds in the bank, back on the beach. Ibrahim and Fatima have renewed their vows with another aerobatic courtship display, and Dylan has introduced us to his new valentine, Sarah, a.k.a. Bob or, as she becomes known, Sarah-bob, his eventual wife. To us, a new daughter.

AFTER OLYMPIA'S MOVE BACK from Australia, I joined John more often on the weekly errands. This resulted in part from John's response to someone asking, "How come we don't see Beatrice in town?"

"She's gone feral," he'd said, "we can't catch her."

So I took on laundromat duties when there were big loads, which thanks to my advance planning didn't happen often. We had plenty of reserve clothing, supplemented on occasion by garments found on the wash-up log by the stream. My everyday river pants, for instance. Upon observing Lolita licking at these with some enthusiasm one day, we agreed on a new laundry scheduling standard. You know it's time to wash your pants when the dog starts doing it for you.

In winter months, the laundromat was pleasantly uncrowded, and I could use five machines at once, which left plenty of town time for wonton soup at Gary's Kitchen, our eatery of choice. Indigenous folk there looked noticeably at ease, happy at the fuss the Chinese owners made over their children.

The fragrance of fresh bread always sucked us into the Common Loaf, which is where we met Phil from Flores, a sculptor and sailor, and also the Catface people. At last, we had found them, convening there over the cold-weather months.

Frank was the elder and central figure. From his favourite seat in the corner, he would spin out a cup of coffee as friends dropped by and chatted. An American expat and former teacher here since

Blending in.

the 1970s, he had initiated and edited Tofino's newspaper *The Sound* and contributed to its successor, *The Sound Magazine*. He also wrote three-act plays. One, *Cougar Annie!*, was on the current program of Tofino's community theatre under the direction of Mister Marx, another Catface regular. Olympia was a cast member.

We were connected by place and by play.

"Drop by at the solstice," Frank said. "We always do a potluck."

ON HER days off, Olympia liked to hang out with us on the island, fishing or working on a quilt for her grandma. She missed the sailboat in Australia, however, and with little thought as to what it would involve, I suggested we build one from beach wood. And it grew from there. We chose a Norwegian sailing dory because it looked easy and manageable for a first attempt. I wrote away for the plans.

When they arrived, we spread them out on the workshop table, and it did not look quite so easy. Before getting into the nitty-gritty, we had to source material. Olympia insisted there be no shortcuts, first class all the way, so we ordered boxes of copper nails with matching roves and bronze ribbed nails of various sizes along with bronze cleats and rowlocks from the best suppliers.

"I'm paying," she insisted.

I already had my eye on a nice, dry red cedar log, and we cut it into half-inch clear planks with the Alaska mill. These we trimmed to width and planed to a quarter inch for hull planks. For the transom, bow plate, and floor planking, we found a massive yellow cedar in a log-jam by the river exit from the forest. I had to cut from both sides with the big saw. For thwarts, spars, and oars, we found perfect tight-grain Sitka spruce, and for the centerboard, rudder, and knees, we dragged out and cut up ancient dead yew from the forest behind the house.

The next step was to cut a plywood mould and set it up on the workshop table. Then began the task of laying the planking. Soon the workshop was ankle deep in curly shavings and the air heavy with the sweet smell of cedar.

Planks were riveted along their length. We drilled, slipped a copper nail through the hole, dropped on a rove, then clipped it off to form a little copper hat. Olympia then supported the back of the nail with a heavy hammer while I tapped the pinched end round and smooth with a riveting hammer.

Tink is born.

After a week of this, the shell was flipped and the plywood mould removed. We worked on the interior frames, using natural curves in the yew to get the right shape for knees and braces. We could not find yew thick enough for broad planks for the rudder and dagger board, so we cut and joined two planks with epoxy. This provided strength and had the added benefit of reduced distortion.

Spars and sweeps rough cut from our slab of Sitka were shaped with a jack plane then finished with sandpaper and spar varnish.

Seeing the boat come together from raw beach material to a gleaming final product felt magical. We painted epoxy inside the shell and dark marine green with white trim on the outside. Olympia ordered a Dacron oxblood-coloured sail from Lunenburg, home of the *Bluenose*.

As we pushed the finished boat out through the waves and dropped the centerboard we felt ridiculously proud of ourselves. Olympia named her *Tink*. She was designed for protected-water sailing and not much use as a West Coast boat, but she sure looked pretty.

THERE WERE memorable happenings between the launch of *Tink* and the solstice: a surreal visit, a deep dive into the past, a newcomer to the family, and a big anniversary calling for Champagne and many Band-Aids.

The visitor

It was our habit to eat our main meal of the day around noon. This was generally followed by an hour's nap. The summer rush of kayakers was about to begin and we were snoozing and contemplating a cuppa tea when there came a loud knock at the door.

"Who the hell is that?" barked the dog. The cats hid.

A fresh-faced young man holding a clipboard stood at the door.

"I'm from Stats Canada and I'm doing the census for the area," he announced.

"You're kidding me."

I glanced past the beach to where an RCMP patrol boat was holding position in the ebbing current.

We brought the young man in and sat him at the table with a cup of tea as we answered his questions and he answered ours. Turns out he was a student and this was a summer gig.

"You're the last along the coast," he said. "I started at Hesquiaht and we're heading back to Tofino today. I stop in at every place I see a cabin where there are signs of life. Some places I'm welcome, others I'm treated like the skunk at the garden party."

The deep dive

ON VICTORIA DAY, we tied up at the Clayoquot Island dock to join the tourist throngs. Stubbs Island, as it is also called, was hosting its annual everyone welcome weekend. There were gardens and forest paths to enjoy, outdoor games for those inclined, layers of history to ponder.

The island was our immediate, tiny neighbour to the east. It lay between us and Tofino, remarkable for its double spit pointing toward Opitsaht. An American heiress had bought it for its beauty in the 1990s and since ceded much of it to the Land Conservancy. Only a master gardener and island manager lived there full-time, off-grid, people we hoped to meet.

The sea otter trade drew the first Europeans into Clayoquot Sound in 1787. Clayoquot Island's colonization began with a trading post in 1855. It was the time between sea otter and seal; the first had been hunted to extinction by then, but the pelagic sealing industry was coming to the fore. The trading post became a proper store, which spawned the area's first colonial settlement. By the turn of the century, the island had a hotel, a school, and a jailhouse. Sealing schooners bound for the Bering Sea stopped there to pick up Nuu-chah-nulth crew, experts at the hunt.

The devastating loss, in 1887, of twenty-four Keltsmaht sealers on a local voyage led to the small Vargas community's joining with their former neighbours, the Ahousaht.[1]

The Vargas homesteaders had filled the vacuum, and the Clayoquot Island store is where the new immigrants provisioned and ordered in the building supplies needed to establish Port Gillam, their own small settlement on Calmus Passage.

As Port Gillam ceased to exist after the First World War, another immigrant settlement appeared, this one right where we stood this holiday Monday on Clayoquot Island. Almost nothing was left of it except for a diffuse sense of loss and regret. It had been a Japanese village, one of four in the area, peopled by fishers skilled at salmon trolling. They and their families had worked hard, settled in, made friends. Then in 1941, the Imperial Japanese Navy Air Service bombed Pearl Harbor and within weeks all Japanese residents on the West Coast were extracted to Hastings Park in Vancouver and from there sent off to distant internment camps. Their fishing boats were confiscated and never returned. Their houses were plundered over time and eventually liquidated by the federal government with the proceeds used to pay the costs of the detention of Japanese Canadians.

Two settlements lost to world wars.

In contrast, fresh life had come to Clayoquot Island in 1940, when two sisters took over the hotel, adding a brew pub and substantial gardens. Their rhododendrons, planted as seeds, had grown sky high: we had to crane our necks to see the tops. We found Frank's companion, Melanie, in a garden patch, standing proud and happy. A former commercial grower, she helped out with the island's upkeep and had family ties to the sisters.

On our way home, we lingered at Port Gillam—it was the little cove with the NO ANCHORAGE sign. There had been a dock here, lost to a storm in the first year. There had been cottages with fenced gardens, a post office, a tiny school for the thirty or so families living or gathering here from other parts of the island.

Everything had melded into the mossy forest. Only sepia photographs, letters, and place names remained, though John's foot hit on something hard as he walked around—a scattered pile of core samples from a mine survey done in recent decades, something we'd heard about. This corner of Vargas and Catface held copper.

Port Gillam owed its name to a well-liked figure, Captain Gillam of the *Princess Maquinna*. From 1913 on, his vessel journeyed up and down the coast from Victoria every ten days, making up to forty stops along the way. The *Princess* brought and picked up mail and cargo, and with fifty staterooms and space for hundreds of day passengers, she was her own village, complete with white tablecloth dining.

Between Clayoquot Island and Port Gillam, she stopped at Kakawis, then occupied by the Christie Indian Residential School. (One of the last such establishments in BC, it has since become a family healing centre.)

At the time of her launching, the *Princess Maquinna* was, at seventy-four metres, the largest steel vessel yet built in BC, and double-hulled to boot. She remained in service until 1953, linking up tiny spots on the map. It was hard to imagine—a funnelled white behemoth chugging up and down Calmus Passage, narrow even to us. Offering tea service. The mind boggled. And yet, she had been not a luxury so much as an essential link to those coastal communities no roads had yet reached, let alone paved ones. (It took until 1971 for a paved road to reach all the way to Tofino.)

The newcomer

It was Fathers' Day when a tall, vivacious redhead walked into our lives. She was around Olympia's age and introduced herself as Kate, a kayak guide on a private trip. On her foot, she sported a martini glass tattoo.

It was lunchtime. She shook down her fiery mane and I poured her a Cuba Libre with demerara rum.

"So how come you're not home on Fathers' Day?" I chided gently.

Her eyes filled with tears.

"My dad died in December," she said. "That's sort of why I'm taking some time."

We all choked up in a group hug, and that day Kate became family.

After she left, Bea and I took our evening walk and found a message written in the sand below high tide: Dad, I miss you.

The anniversary

June 19 was our thirtieth. Something special was in order. We had bubbly, a pile of prawns (a gift from Vince), some freshly shelled crab, and the makings for a salad that would do credit to the Chelsea Flower Show. But something was missing.

"We need to do something special…something we haven't done before," I suggested.

Bea gave me an anxious look.

"Why don't we take the trail to the summit then walk on a compass course to Ahous?" I said.

She looked almost relieved.

"Alright, then," she said simply, "it's a plan." Then, "Do we have the topo map for that area?"

"Nah, it's okay, we'll just take a bearing from the summit."

We stuffed snack food and water bottles into a backpack together with a change of clothing, a VHF radio, and a first aid kit. I carried my Japanese bush knife and a pocket full of hard caramels, and we set off past the emergency cabin with Lolita charging ahead.

The first forty minutes of hiking was fairly straightforward, though it being June, the day-mosquitoes were out. We had not done that walk since the previous fall, and the path had already closed over in places. It mostly avoided the soggy parts but with a few spectacular exceptions that required crawling beneath fresh windfalls and crossing streams that were higher and boggier than we remembered.

As we walked, I swished my bush knife, trimming back the salal and huckleberry that leaned into the open space of the trail. After twenty minutes, we came out into the big clearing.

By eleven o'clock, we stood on the summit, glancing back the way we had come. To the west lay the open ocean with its small green islands. Lacy spume trailed seaward with the ebbing current. A fishing boat appeared, beating its way toward Tofino. I took a bearing due south to the gleaming white crescent of Ahous Bay and eyeballed a ridge that roughly followed our course. After a swig of water and a cookie, we set off.

We knew that walking off-trail was going to be tough but the ferocity of the resistance astonished us. What to do…push the salal and huckleberry branches aside, crawl under them, crawl over them, or hack a trail through? Basically, we did it all in about that order. Where we could, we walked around the nastiest thickets, but they usually occurred in gullies where there was a risk that deviating from our course too much might get us deflected. Sometimes the easiest path meant climbing trees on cliffs.

For two hours, we pushed, hacked, and crawled our way through ever more resistant thickets. Sometimes we glimpsed the sea,

Hope.

though we never again saw Ahous. As the terrain started to slope downwards more frequently than it sloped up, we made encouraging noises to each other. Occasionally we came upon mossy clearings threaded with tiny rivulets that parted and rejoined beneath the moss. Here, the going was easier and we made better time, striding along, holding course nicely.

Abruptly the ground gave way beneath my left foot and I dropped into a narrow trench, cracking my knee on a rock on the way down. A fierce pain shot up my leg and I cursed so explosively that Lolita thought it was her fault and ran behind Beatrice.

Even before I had pulled my leg from the hole, I'd figured it was going to be near impossible to get a rescue chopper in with all the standing dead cedar spikes crowded around us. In agony, I rolled over onto the moss as Bea approached gingerly, worried. Hastily, I ran my hands down my leg, relieved to find it was still roughly the shape I remembered. No bones were protruding, though waves of pain swept up from a rapidly swelling spot beside my knee.

"Here, lie back and take a rest," Bea said.

"If I do, you'll have to carry me out," I snarled, and crawled to my feet. She tried to take my arm but I shook her off impatiently. I was such a jerk when I was hurting, but she was used to that. I stumbled on, cursing and slashing at the undergrowth with renewed vigour.

Interest in reaching Ahous evaporated. The important thing now was to get home while I could still walk. Bea too was starting to stumble and at one point pulled up her trouser cuffs to reveal shins battered blue from her knees to the tops of her hiking boots. We looked at each other and laughed.

"Happy anniversary," I said. We shifted course to the southwest to pick up the coast trail.

It took less than an hour of floundering through swamp to come out on the well-trodden path. Relief was front and centre as we swung right without stopping, limping stiff-legged through old-growth giants, past Fingers, then Dunes and Little Baja, before re-entering the forest for the last two miles to home beach.

It was almost five o'clock when we staggered out of the trees, laughing light-headedly. We'd not made it to Ahous but we'd given it a pretty good try. Arm in arm, we stumbled across the beach to our prawns and waiting Champagne.

The solstice

WE KNEW WHICH HOUSE to head to for our solstice visit—the one with the blue-framed windows at Island beach. We'd been quite late setting off, and by the time our bow crunched onto the sloping beachfront the guests were dispersing: a yacht was in position to pick up a babbling load of friends, shuttled over by canoe in ones and twos. Small powerboats jostled pleasantly on their way out.

Dry suits unzipped to the waist, we mingled with the friends remaining—close kin and neighbours of the sort who would help clean up and debrief quietly after what might well be Frank's last solstice. He was old now, and emphysema had a tight grip on him. Thus, there was a touch of solemnity in the air.

Neighbours Karedwyn and Paul stood by, attuned to the moment. She, a metaphysical counsellor, must have twigged to our interest in mushrooms because she immediately let us in on a secret chanterelle patch on our side of the channel.

By this summer's start, we had a reasonable sense of who was who on Catface. John had met Lloyd the Architect in town. His was the high-perched house with the cantilevered dock. Through Olympia, we had connected with young Sam and Clay, both of whom had ties to the two-cabin beach as did Sam's dad, a woodturner and sculptor well-known for his massive burl masks. Two more Catface folk we knew through Dawson. They were a jumble of Yanks, Brits, Ontarians, and one Turk. In summer, it made for a lively neighbourhood.

Kal from next door was currently absent, but was mentioned as a suspect in the disappearance of some of Melanie's tomato seedlings. She would get to the bottom of it.

The vegetable garden was otherwise shaping up very nicely, with trellises ready for broad beans and a pleasantly loose orderliness to the seaside patch. The ornamental garden was small but sweet, memorable to me for its dwarf rhododendron. There was little flat ground behind the house, but enough water from a mountain stream to run a mini turbine.

Frank took pride in the house he had built decades before, a substantial shake-clad cottage with a bay window. Although it was technically a squat on Crown Land, "I pay taxes on this every year," Frank had stated with obvious satisfaction. (Legacy status: if you can't fight them, tax them.)

Catface in our summer lagoon.

Inside, the house had the spare look one expects of dwellings left over winter. The walls were bare except for one painting upstairs. Objects were returning, though—the worktable at the rear of the open kitchen was well stocked with tools. The house had an indoor bathtub, we noted.

We sat at the kitchen table and chatted amiably between bites; before us lay platters of the greatest leftovers. A solstice well celebrated, however late we had arrived.

Frank died the following year. Kal and a friend built a magnificent box for him, as well as for other neighbours when their time came. Frank's body journeyed to Tofino in Marcel's herring skiff and, once at the dock, was transferred to the back of a pickup truck for the trip to the hospital morgue. There was a heartfelt memorial walk after the shock had passed.

About Frank, boats, cougars, and bears

THE YEAR OF HIS last solstice Frank published *Journeys: Stories from Clayoquot Sound*, a collection of short works illustrated by his close and longtime friend Joanna (Joanna of the floathouse, and formerly of Catface).

We learned from Frank's recollections of thirty-five years that time matters. It does in simple ways, as it did when he set up a vigil, one July day, to record all the boats going past his house (large or small, inbound or outbound) over a twenty-four hour period (seventeen of daylight). The result was astounding: 246.

"There is, especially during summer, hardly a minute of daylight when no boats are visible," he wrote. Calmus Passage was a busy place.

Time matters in complicated ways as well, and sometimes it stops, or it slows to the point where you can't breathe. As when Frank had gone searching for his nine-year-old son in the woods behind the house, and the awful truth began to dawn that a cougar had taken the child, that the child would not survive.

A story we had heard but not wanted to believe.

It was a trauma Frank had lived with for eighteen years, the memory ticking daily inside his head.

COUGARS ARE numerous on the Vancouver Island mainland and its Catface extension. They also roam Flores Island, taking dogs from the Maaqtusiis Reserve. Campers are advised to keep dogs at home or on a leash. Kayak groups at Chetarpe on Catface, or Whitesands Beach on Flores, two favourite campsites, have to keep careful watch. Juveniles have been spotted in Tofino sometimes, lounging on tree branches overlooking the elementary school.

Settler Cougar Annie had been famous for shooting them; she tethered goats out as cougar bait. She did well from the skins and provincial bounty, and the meat she likely bottle-preserved as it is reportedly quite sweet.

From the book *Cougar Annie's Garden* by Margaret Horsfield:

> "Sometimes when Cougar Annie tethered a goat out as cougar bait, she would stay alert well into the night, listening for it to start bleating with fear. As soon as she heard the goat bleat she would go out armed with a lantern and her gun. She killed many cougars at night. According to some stories, she was able to take aim, shoot, and kill a cougar without even putting the lantern down."[2]

In cougar country, there were bears aplenty as well, especially when the salmon came upriver. Bear watching tours came as a seasonal option to Tofino tourists.

Though wolves could be a menace on Vargas, we had only them to contend with.

Of ravens and men

The breakfast dance Bea developed with Fatima and Ibrahim fostered trust, but the birds still kept their distance, prancing sideways, wary, springing into the air at the first hint of a trap or bad intent. To advance the relationship, Bea took to adding a marshmallow to the menu. It became the prize worth a mouthful of mice.

The ravens soon figured that kayak campers were an alternate source of marshmallows, but they would have to steal them. So, when I came across a party of kids throwing sticks at something out of reach up a tree, I had a fair idea of what had happened. There was Ibrahim with a whole bag of marshmallows. He had pecked a hole in the plastic and with one claw holding the bag against the branch, was delicately picking them out for immediate consumption. I'd warned the kids about thieving ravens, so they had shoved the unopened bag up beyond the footrests inside a kayak. Ibrahim bided his time then hopped inside the boat, dragged the bag out and got airborne with it for a low-level victory pass.

These were birds in command of their territory, likely quite old. They had seen different folks come and go over the years, some friendly, some not. They had a lot of tricks. They chased off marauding eagles, entire murders of crows, and other ravens eyeing their territory. Though often joyous, life was a battle. This year they had produced no chicks, or maybe the wet winter killed them.

Lolita chased them any chance she got. They would see her coming and nonchalantly hop onto a beach stump just out of reach. Sometimes they would lead her out onto the open beach, flying just beyond her nose, then turn the tables, suddenly looping over to peck her back, just in front of her tail, the one spot she could not reach.

A favourite (natural) food for the ravens was the leathery mermaid's purse or egg case containing young skate that sometimes washed ashore after a storm. Early one morning, we noticed Ibrahim pecking at something on the beach while Fatima stood by, waiting for whatever he could not eat or carry away. As we approached, they backed off. They had pecked a hole in the purse and pulled out a perfectly formed baby skate with two round dots like eyes on its back. It was still wriggling in the albumen that had spilled from the case. Bea picked it up and put it in the sea. To our amazement, it set off swimming strongly for open water.

I slit the purse open with my knife. Half a dozen young skates with identical markings writhed vigorously inside. We took the egg case to the water's edge and submerged it. As the sea flooded their incubator, they floated free, all swimming for open water.

"I think we owe the ravens extra mice," Bea said as we walked home.

Sounds of the sound

Noise was a surprising feature of Vargas summers. Our house was on a direct line between Tofino and Hot Springs and floatplanes flew just a few hundred metres above the treetops. *Whoosh! Roar!*

Skate mermaid's purse
with beach currency.

Tink takes on the Pacific.

You'd stand up suddenly and whack your head or hit your thumb with a hammer. Then there was noise from spotter planes and the whale-watching and sport fishing boats. It was an integral part of summer. We were, however, spared much of the traffic Frank had tallied from his beach. The speedboats from the fish farms, the workboats, the tugboats, the scheduled sea bus, and water taxis to Ahousaht or Hot Springs—none of these went past us.

One sound we shared with Catface folk was the throb of the abominable *Leviathan II*, which we could hear long before the boat appeared. Best viewed from a great distance, the monstrosity occasionally surprised us by coming between us and Burgess, where, to our amazement, it cleared the sandbar.

Sailboats, though easy on the ear, were rare on our side of Vargas and the few that visited did not linger long; our anchorages were iffy at best. One particular sailboat, a small sloop, paused overnight on its way around Vancouver Island. On board were Greg, a now familiar kayak instructor, his wife Jolie, who wrote for *Pacific Yachting*, and their two kids, a small boy and a baby girl.

We let them loose in the garden for the greens they craved.

Tink, our own sailing vessel, had acquitted herself well upon launching, propelled by oar or sail. The few adjustments required were performed in the fair waters of our seasonal lagoon. On one occasion, however, *Tink* did take fright, heading toward Flores at great speed, looking lovely under full sail but much in need of a tow back to home beach.

Fish, fish, and more fish

Migrating salmon passed our beach on their way to the rivers of their birth. There, those that made it spawned and died. First to arrive were the bluebacks, foot-long, vigorous, good eating fish that swam in dark schools past Eby into Calmus Passage. We mostly caught them from the rocks at either end of the beach, but also by wading into the water off the main beach and from a small beach that appeared at low tide beyond the northern rocks, facing Catface. This we named Sometimes beach. It had to be the fabled fishing hole, we decided. Here, the current carved a kelp-free channel close to shore and we could cast into the flow.

Salmon, hot-smoked
with green alder.

Once the main runs of coho started to come through, we'd need the wheelbarrow to carry the fish home. I would clean and fillet them at a cutting table in front of the boathouse, attended by two ravens and the house menagerie. I'd cut the fillets into chunks, keep the choice bits for lunch, then cure the rest with a mixture of coarse salt and brown sugar. The pieces were allowed to weep dry, then placed in the smoker, a home-built affair created from a large propane tank with layers of stainless racks and a controllable firebox for alder chips. The aroma of salmon curing in wood smoke made the dogs drool. When the fish was firm and cured, the pieces were vacuum-bagged and frozen.

Fresh, we preferred our salmon cooked on a charcoal barbeque or a scorching hot, ridged pan, then sprinkled with rock salt and freshly ground black pepper, topped at the last moment with butter. Usually, we accompanied it with a dill mayonnaise thinned with lemon juice, or we'd melt dill butter onto the hot fillet at serving then squeeze on fresh lemon. Bea usually claimed the tail, I got the thicker bits, and we fought over the bellies and cheeks. For variety, we'd sometimes rub an entire fillet with chili seasoning mix in oil and grill. The secret was to never overcook . . . just enough so the flesh remained moist with a hint of translucence and the outside was slightly charred.

Food became a daily celebration. We'd give each meal a rating out of ten based on flavour, timing, texture, and presentation.

Rockfish, ling cod, and perch we considered the equals of salmon, usually lightly poached in seawater, sprinkled with parsley and a little butter at serving. Occasionally we fried them in a beer batter but we both preferred them egg-dipped and coated with flour or breadcrumbs.

I thrived on the excitement of fishing, of watching the surface for those telltale swirls, then casting to the most likely spot and teasing the lure back to the beach, always ready for that "big hit." My preferred lure for salmon evolved to a ten-centimetre Buzz Bomb with the triple hook cluster replaced by a yellow, green, or blue bucktail fly. It swam like a fish and had enough weight to be carried well out.

Early morning and dusk were my favourite times, when the light was soft and the hills a pale pastel. The fish were coming by all day but they seemed more willing to take the lure during those times. Maybe they liked the shifting shadows of the hills and the reflections through the water too. Or maybe they just couldn't see as well.

When my sister Judith and her hubbie, Dene, came to visit from New Zealand, he chartered Björn, a local guide, and his well-appointed sport fishing boat for a day. At last, I got to ride around in circles like all those boats I'd watched off Burgess. Björn was the go-to guide for other guides. He knew where the big fish were likely to be and what lure to use that day. And he was generous with his knowledge.

Trolling with downriggers, flashers, and plugs was something I'd never done before. It was new and exciting. I stood out of the way and watched as Björn attached a flasher and turquoise plug, then dropped the lead ball to eighteen metres, where the image of a school of salmon appeared in the fish finder. Every move he made oozed a competence born of familiarity. After a few minutes, the first fish hit. Björn handed Dene the rod while he worked the boat to keep pressure on the line. Dene reeled in the first of several nice springs. Björn scooped them up in the net and dropped them in the fish well. It did not take long to reach our limit and Dene beamed all the way home.

Oddly, salmon caught by sport fishers were normally cleaned at the dock, frozen, then shipped to a Nanaimo cannery. Dene received his salmon in tins months later in New Zealand.

One afternoon, I was back at the northern rocks, casting toward Eby without success when my lure seemed to hook the bottom. Maybe a big fish? I often thought "big fish" when I hooked a wad of kelp, but this felt different. I gave the line a tug to free it and whatever it was took off.

Line whizzed out. Rod bent hard over. Adrenalin rushed. I gently tightened the drag. That did nothing to slow the run. Mist from the speeding line hovered around the reel. It felt like I'd hooked a passing torpedo and I envied Björn being able to follow a fish when it ran. The amount of line on the spool shrank fast. Colour change told me I was beyond the normal amount of run line and into reserve. And still the big fish ran. I remembered a tip from a guide and banged the rod with my left hand. The shock ran down the line and the fish paused. Then off it went again. Two hundred metres out to sea a huge spring salmon leapt clear of the water,

Company at the rock.

Clockwise from top left: a prize catch; a mighty bolete; chanterelles as we liked them; and Dylan hunting stumps.

my line attached. Now the adrenalin was really pumping. The fish started to run again.

The reel was loaded with about three hundred metres of very thin, very strong, and very expensive synthetic woven line and I figured it was almost all used up. When it reached the end, the line or the hook would snap. I had to slow the run and start bringing the fish in. I bumped the rod again, harder this time, and to my relief the fish stopped. I pulled back on the rod and reclaimed a few metres of line, but it was all from the rod. The fish had not moved.

The standoff continued, me pulling, fish resisting. Then it started to move again, this time to the right and I was able to gain some line, feeling more optimistic with every metre back on the reel. Then off he went again (I'd decided it was a "he"). Line whizzed. A tour boat came into my narrow field of vision and I yelled and tried to wave them away. They waved back. The fish must have dived as the boat passed over because the feared dead line did not occur. The boat cruised on and the big fish jumped again, astern of the boat this time. The tourists cheered.

I leaned into the rod, clawing line back, metre by metre. Then I'd wait as the fish pulled. The drag was as tight as I dared. There was wear near the hook so I had to go easy. I lost track of time.

"Easy old boy," I said aloud.

The fish ran again, powerfully, out to sea, but not so far this time and he came back more easily. We were both getting tired. Off he ran again.

"Now, turn, turn," I coaxed.

The fish turned.

A small crowd had gathered on the rocks. Flores and McKay turned from mauve to indigo. The bronze side of the big spring glowed as it glided by, leaning against the hook just fifteen metres from shore. Now the runs were smaller, thirty metres, fifteen metres. Hold. Then, ever so gently, he gave up. I felt remorse as I drew that beautiful perfect fish into a narrow cove. I waded into the water and slipped my fingers behind its gills. Exhausted, I dragged it up onto the beach and dispatched it with a blow. The hook fell onto the sand.

AROUND THE end of September, Mel's beach hosts the remnant of what was once the massive Atleo River sockeye run. The narrow

We had more success getting food from clam beds than the garden beds on our beach. Although nice greens did emerge from the seaweed, drought and windblown sand soon made tending them futile. The beach grasses, meanwhile, made up their own garden.

channel between Vargas Island and Hobbs Islet used to be known as "salmon alley" because when the salmon were running, old timers told of fin-to-fin fish as millions swam through. For many centuries prior, the run provided for the Ahousaht People and for the Otsosaht People before them. Now, what is left provides sport for wealthy fly-in fishers.

I discovered the remnants by accident when I noticed jumpers weeks after the coho run had finished. Curious, I went back for my rod and cast into the bay. I hooked a type of salmon I had not seen in those parts. It was slimier than a coho with a more elongated body shape. The meat was a darker red, excellent eating. I took a sample to Vince. An ex-commercial fisher, he confirmed it was indeed a sockeye, explaining that in four consecutive years, seiners had been allowed to scoop the entire Atleo run as they awaited rain to swim the river. What I was seeing were genocide survivors.

Water and watercraft

Going into the Labour Day weekend, Tofino declared its Meares Island reservoir nearly empty. Resorts and businesses were asked to shut down to conserve water. Environment Canada observed, in its Top Ten Weather Stories for 2006: "How ironic that the picturesque community by the sea was enjoying its best weather in memory, only to be closed down by a summer-long drought."

Marlin and Mary (M&M) came to spend a week in September, as they had the previous year. Marlin was a grouch and a master of deadpan; Mary, composed and competent, did a good job of keeping him in line. They ran a big paddle sports business in Abbotsford, both as retailers and manufacturers. Once business competitors, we had become Boat Show friends. Then real friends. Dylan and I had stayed at their cabin in the Chilcotin, fishing for sweet-tasting trout one summer, and another time we all paddled the Harrison River to see the salmon run.

On their first visit, Marlin had viewed our water supply with suspicion.

"It's collected off a clean steep roof," I said. "No creosote."

"Birds poop on roofs," he said.

"True, but it is filtered through moss."

Marlin was unconvinced.

So this visit, he had brought a water testing kit along with samples of commercially bottled water and a drum of water that had passed through the fancy purification system at his house. We tested them all. Vargas water, despite the drought, was the purest. The least pure was the store-bought bottled water. He was vexed.

Marlin was a gear freak, and he and Mary were generous with wondrous gifts from their shop and from Marlin's online prowling: bright battery lights, waterproof bags, and marvellously, a set of sturdy canoe wheels to replace the jury-rigged cart I had built.

The gift of which Marlin was most proud this year, however, was a new toilet seat with a foam cover, decorated with tropical shell designs. It was to replace the cold one we'd found on the beach still in its packaging. Unfortunately, the field mice also liked it, nibbling the foam and dragging bits off for their nests.

Marlin was not a fan of our outhouse, and he was disconcerted by our sign on the paper bag beside the seat: SOILED PAPER HERE. WE RECYCLE.

"Come on, Marlin, it's a joke."

When it came to canoes, M&M were true believers. This time, I had met them at the water's edge as they turned up with a particularly pretty, yellow canoe.

"Boy, you're lucky to make it all the way out here in that dodgy little boat," I said.

Marlin rose to the bait.

"You'd be surprised the seas I've been in, in this canoe," he said.

"Maybe with a spray cover," I said, grimacing. "Too much windage, I'd have thought—of course, you could always put on a rudder."

Marlin scowled.

"They handle just fine when you learn how to paddle. Maybe I can show you one day."

After much badgering he eventually got me to try out the yellow canoe, taking care I wore a life jacket, though I explained I had no intention of going beyond my depth. Bungie came along. *Click! Click!* And there it was—Marlin had the cover for next year's catalogue. "A new convert to canoeing," read the eventual caption.

Canoes had a checkered history in our area, with some epic journeys recorded by the Catface folk, among others, and rescues to match.

A death defying excursion in a strange craft.

The argument that they were strictly protected-water craft was often outweighed by their more attractive price compared to kayaks.

Not that people didn't come to grief in kayaks. They certainly did and probably in the same proportions, just in different conditions. Bea had been traumatized by the accident reports she'd had to edit in our quarterly, particularly a fatality off Rafael Point, the crux of the outside route to Hot Springs.

Risk is a funny thing. The concept of "risk homeostasis" is that we adjust our behaviour to our level of comfort with risk. Safety improvements mean we can do more risky things while the relative risk we are willing to accept remains constant … the risk threshold. Survival depends on our ability to make these assessments, and toying with the risk threshold is what provides the thrill for adrenalin junkies.

One of the joys of beach life.

Two examples, these involving inflatables. Though the personally acceptable level of risk is a constant, the hazard factor may appear much higher to a bystander. In the first instance, Dylan was coming back with Olympia and a girlfriend around New Year's. The friend's flight from Vancouver had been delayed, so by the time they left Tofino, it was already dark. It was also stormy with big swells and a high tide. Dylan and Olympia wore dry suits and the friend a surfing wetsuit. He radioed ahead with an ETA and to check on beach conditions. Soon, a little white light bobbed around off the beach appearing and disappearing in the swells. When they came in, it was at high speed atop a surge wild as a mountain river. As soon as they touched the sand everyone jumped out, pumped up on adrenalin, and we all rushed the boat up the ramp.

"Well, that was exciting," Olympia said.

In the other example, Sarah-bob was with us for Thanksgiving and the kids all wanted to get to town for another turkey feast at Sarah's parents'. Once again, the surf was large and unruly and Bea was having a litter of kittens as we four sat on the tubes warming up the motor and waiting for the break. She stood in the waves holding the bow, then, looking Sarah square in the eyes, said "You don't have to do this, you know." Sarah, who had limited experience in boats at that stage, took her cue from the rest of us. Dylan and Olympia were raring to go. She accepted the risk threshold of the rest of us (as we do when we board a passenger plane).

"I'm sure we'll be fine," Sarah said.

"There it is!" I called.

Bea stepped aside as we blasted out through a soft spot. The swells were large, smooth, and easy offshore. I glanced back at the beach and could see Bea standing on a high stump, waiting for survivors. We flew past Eby and rushed with the waves up Calmus.

Back in the day, the Trade Association of Sea Kayakers (TASK) watched anxiously as cheap plastic boats were introduced in big-box stores. These were sold with no buoyancy, spray covers, or guidance on how to use them and we braced for the worst, expecting bodies washing ashore all over North America. It didn't happen. We had underestimated the common sense of the common person. People realized they were dealing with a toy, not a serious boat, and they adjusted their behaviour.

Safety in small boats was always a preoccupation of mine. It meant exploring that risk threshold and had led to the book, the magazine, the TASK guidelines, and the videos. It kept me awake many nights thinking about the young couple from Victoria who died off Race Rocks in a boat we had sold them, and the mother who came to tell me her son had been inspired by my book then died "doing what he loved to do" in heavy surf off the Oregon coast.

Rainy season

That fall, Olympia moved into a Tofino apartment with two roommates and dropped Bungie off with us.

"She'd be much happier with you guys," she declared.

We were delighted. The rains had returned in earnest by then, so Bungie arrived in an oiled-cotton, fleece-lined Australian raincoat with a high collar that made her look even more bat like. But being shorthaired and small, she could use the extra layer, at least till she acclimatized.

Our Aussie canine took well to the wild, wet weather but did not like wading the river where cold water lapped at her belly. Instead, she would wait to be picked up, and if that failed, try and hop across on two legs. Which two legs seemed to vary. She did not enjoy swimming. As a puppy, she had fallen off the anchored sailboat during the night. Fortunately, Olympia, hearing an

Autumn squall.

right Doing battle
with creosote.

unusual sound, had gone on deck with her headlamp and seen a glint of eyes at the limit of its range. She set off by kayak to rescue the poor thing, who by then was barely able to keep her head up, her stomach all agurgle with seawater.

BEA TORE October and November off the kitchen calendar. We'd been on the beach more than two full years. We had learned about dory building, about catching crabs, salmon, and rockfish, about feathered visitors, neighbours, mushrooms, storm surges, and how to paddle a canoe on dead flat water. We had learned the difference between great tasting garlic and ordinary garlic—our first crop of Russian Red was stellar.

The learning curve on weather and waves was steep and nuanced. This year's weather weirdness had destabilized everyone. Was this some kind of new normal for the West Coast?

What we knew for certain was that in summer, enough sand was piled on the beach that we could leave the boat beyond the lagoon; in winter, we knew to bring it up as high as we could.

All in all, we were getting a reasonable handle on routines.

There were small routines like the spring beating of the Turkish carpet to get rid of the sand, digging compost into garden beds, and for Bea, the pleasant ongoing ritual of polishing the stove.

Maintaining motors and tools was something I enjoyed. It felt very Zen to have the chainsaw up on the workbench, filing each tooth methodically at the perfect angle with the optimal number of strokes.

We kept fuel in numbered twenty-litre containers and cycled through to minimize deterioration while still keeping enough on hand for an emergency.

There was the bimonthly epic of cleaning the creosote from the chimney, in particular the crust of carbon that closed off the cap. Sometimes there was nothing for it but to climb onto the steep roof and brush out the pipes, but when only the cap was encrusted I could shoot it clean with a pellet gun. It left a few dents on the cap, but as Bea pointed out, "Better its cap than yours."

On and off, Bea worked to consolidate an old metal dump pile I had found in the bushes behind the tractor's new resting spot—squashing ancient, rust-eaten refuse into a compact, less disturbing mound.

ON DECEMBER 14–15 a severe
wind and rain storm batters
the West Coast, with winds
of 185 kilometres per hour
(115mph) recorded at Estevan
lighthouse on the Hesquiaht
peninsula. Vancouver's Stanley
Park is devastated and a
quarter of a million house-
holds are without power.

WE HUNKERED down and watched Brabant Channel turn white,
driving waves over the north rocks. During a pause in the rain, we
went onto the beach to stand in eye-watering wind that tore at our
clothes and drove the occasional raindrop through like pinpricks.

In the sloppy, sloshing calm after the storm, Dylan went to
town in the inflatable to pick up Olympia and her roommate Kristi.
The storm surge had floated hundreds of logs into the surf zone.
These combined with debris from flooded rivers to provide a surf
obstacle course. Dylan brought the boat in through the breakers, dodging logs and flotsam, yet Kristi stepped ashore unfazed,
entirely unaware of what she had been through because she had
taken her glasses off to avoid flying spray.

THE HIGHLIGHTS of Christmas holidays were always the family beach walks. Winter storms meant fresh treasures every morning, mostly flotsam from fish farms or floats that broke away from set nets far out in the Pacific. This year, we found a pill box with a Spanish label. It contained a copper sailmaker's needle and thread, and three coins, one from Chile, one from Australia, and one from China. This was the time of year we found the exotic vodka bottles, one with etched designs on the glass and a necklace of barnacles along for the ride. Or one, less exotic but of a certain vintage, containing a neatly worded message with an invitation to meet up for coffee sometime; it had a Kitsilano phone number, no longer in use.

One day, the bus company called to say a package was waiting for us. In fact, there were *two* plastic canoe buckets with bright-coloured screw lids come from Abbotsford, filled with Christmas goodies for us and the animals, and a range of gadgets including a laser pointer for the cats and an electric badminton racquet for mosquitoes.

"There's a bug on your nose."

Bea kept still as I approached and carefully touched the intruder. Bea's eyes watered and a hatch pattern appeared on the tip of her nose.

The toy was confiscated.

On Boxing Day, she, Olympia, Dylan, and Sarah-bob were walking both dogs on Mel's beach. I stayed behind briefly to make a phone call from the point with my recently acquired smartphone. Judging from the level of agitation when I rejoined them, I had missed some drama.

"Two wolves came out of the forest halfway down the beach," Bea explained. "Both dogs took off after them. One was jet black and *unbelievably* big. They were both whirling and snapping as Bungie ran around and 'round them."

Olympia, who was clutching Bungie when I arrived, had apparently given a banshee scream, and taken off to join the melee in full attack mode.

"What on earth were you thinking?" I asked.

"I don't know. I'd wrestle them or something."

"With your bare hands?"

Russian vodka. One day, against all odds, a barnacle-encrusted lightbulb and neon tube floated in from Japan.

top Spook-dog visitation.

bottom A fresh tuft of red-string seaweed (*Sarcodiotheca gaudichaudii*).

"I never heard a human make a sound like that," Bea said.

"I don't wonder they ran away," said Dylan. "I would have too."

Meanwhile, Lolita was somewhere in the forest barking. When she emerged she was strutting with pride, and the wolves howling to reunite.

"That was the Jack Russell instinct in Bungie," our Aussie friend Carlton later explained. "The wolf was lucky. A Russell will run around a wolf till they get a chance to duck under its belly and slash it open, then they keep circling till the wolf gets tangled in its own entrails." After that explanation we viewed our little lapdog somewhat differently. It also explained an occasion when Cobber had tried to retrieve his tennis ball from a thieving Jack Russell. After circling Cobber repeatedly, the Russell dropped the ball, then dived under Cobber's belly when he went to pick it up. Then it stood back watching. We later discovered a long, red, skin-deep slash from one side of his belly to the other.

The haircut

Olympia's hair had changed hues in recent months. Someone she knew at the Tofino hair salon had sought to expand her colour palette through experimentation and found in her a willing subject. Results had been intriguing but undramatic until this latest outcome—a disturbing maroon none of us could bear.

"Babou, help me cut it off," she pleaded.

Sarah-bob recoiled, not aware hair cutting was a tradition in our family. I always cut Bea's hair and she mine (such as it is), and Dylan (Babou) had cut my hair, once, when he was eight. The plan was for a gamine haircut, which required scissors, then the use of a new cordless hair clipper Dylan happened to have in his bag. He proceeded cautiously, but apparently at the wrong setting, leaving a sizable bald streak on the left hemisphere.

We'd seen our daughter in many roles over her short but intense ballet career, but this was Joan of Arc after the English got to her.

"Really?" said Bea, still sporting her nose grid.

Sarah-bob sat down.

"Well," Olympia said to her mirror and her wide-eyed sibling, "Let's make it look intentional then. Shave it all off!"

He buzzed away tremulously until his work was done.

There was silence.

Once we had shaken off the death-camp, cancer-ward, and neo-Nazi associations, Bea and I were forced to recognize the obvious—before us was a perfectly shaped cranium, as round and smooth as a lightbulb. One we had never seen as Olympia newborn had been well tufted. We had a brand new daughter; our third in a year.

And it starts in the wee hours.

5

THE EXPERTS

SPRING BROUGHT THE RAUCOUS sounds of young ravens as Ibrahim and Fatima shuttled whacked mice and food scraps to their hidden brood. At least they had success this year.

When the chicks fledged, we had the dubious honour of seeing them brought to our place for babysitting. On our roof, they would be safe from eagles. We benefited because crows stayed away from our garden. The screeching, however, began at 4:00 AM, right above our bed. It got easier when they got dropped off on the workshop roof instead—not as steep and easier for us to watch. We gave the ravens' alert call, four CAWS, whenever anything was amiss, and the parents turned up right away.

The other spring regulars were rufous hummingbirds drinking from the feeder at our sunroom window. It was common to see ten or more of them battling for the single nipple of sweet water. Dawson filmed them using the slow motion feature of his camera. On replay, we saw how they used their claws to run up the back of the bird at the nipple, then bump it out of the way in a free-for-all. Both cats watched, chins vibrating.

We had added to the menagerie with four plump Barred Plymouth Rock hens, purchased from a breeder near Coombs. I built them a fenced area with an elevated house where they could escape from predators, and in return, they presented us with four perfect warm eggs each day.

Our early-bird kayak group, the Coastal Adventure Tourism class, appeared during a protracted stormy period. I visited a soggy, saggy series of well-rigged tarps on the sandy bench,

mid-beach, and found a group of ten trainees standing grim-faced under a main tarp with water almost up to their knees. Nobody had ever known that area to flood. They held soggy notebooks on which they attempted note-taking with soggy pencils. Meanwhile, their guest instructor, Michael, my nemesis of past years, was standing just inside the tarp, dodging discharges of roof water while reading from a textbook he had written.

Michael and I had opposing views on the merits of paddler certification. I was against, convinced that certification programs would change the nature of sea kayaking and leave it open to self-serving and exclusive commercial interests. It would have the effect of turning it from a freedom activity to a "belonging" activity.

"Having fun?" I enquired. Then, without waiting for the affirmative chorus, "Would you prefer to do this in our guest cabin? It

Vanier High students help bring in firewood.

opposite Barred Plymouth Rock hens: good-natured and steady layers.

Alder rounds ready for the maul.

has a cozy little wood stove." I looked over to Michael, who rolled his eyes and laughed in resignation. His students were already bolting for their tents to get stuff to dry.

When I checked in on the guest cabin later that morning, there was a sauna party. Steam rose from sodden sleeping bags and wet clothing lay draped over bunks. The wood stove glowed a dull red and everyone was down to underwear. Outside, rain continued to drive across the beach, lashing the forest. The river had flooded and a thin sheet of water spread across the sand. Michael was happy, though there was way too much laughter to learn lessons.

Lolita was thrilled with the improved social scene and looked after them for the duration—until the arrival of the next group, Vanier High.

Mel turned up for the annual visit, with his wife on this occasion. We saw their boat go by and met them at their beach. Sheryl stepped ashore wearing turquoise high-heeled sandals and a fashionable scarf across her shoulder.

Mel liked the improvements, and Sheryl said our place looked even prettier than in Dick and Jane's day—high praise. As they were leaving, Mel suggested that instead of paying rent, we maintain the gardens on his side of the property. How perfect. We could put to rest the beach garden experiment.

Mel had commented on a tall hemlock with a foot-wide trunk that was leaning toward his tower at an angle of forty-five degrees. It needed to be felled. If I cut it at the base with a chainsaw, it would damage the house. The solution was to bring it down in two parts, but there were no low branches, and my days of climbing monkey-style were long gone. I grabbed the rifle and a box of shells and, taking care spent bullets would do no damage, started shooting at a point halfway along the trunk, on the underside. The first two shots served as an undercut. Then I started down from the top, firing ten more rounds, each one incrementally lower. Each shot took its toll till the top sagged and fell softly beside the house.

Bea welcomed our new responsibilities.

I HAD MY DOUBTS about John's Brutalist approach to landscaping, but hard work was called for to get the new gardens ready for a crop. The prospect delighted me; I had long eyed the potential of that twin set of low raised beds by the workshop, fallow for ages but sunny

enough and well protected from wind. Some herbs still grew there. The soil just needed a good forking over and a feed of compost.

Mel loved gardens. His face lit up whenever the topic arose. He'd been amused at a charming little plant I'd stolen from his side and displayed in a clay pot by the Appendix.

"Where'd you find that?" he said. "It's a terrible weed I introduced accidentally bringing in planters from Victoria. I can't get rid of the darn thing."

Herb Robert. My plant book had said good things about it, and it did look pretty, but alas it deserved its common name, "Stinky Bob," and was such an invader I'd have to rip it all out from behind his disused lower greenhouse, a hopeless task as it turned out. Mel's patch of oxeye daisies, another invader, was from homesteader days, he said. It was limited to a sunny spot near the beach.

I put in a row of veggies around the inside perimeter of the greenhouse and encouraged a few raspberry canes visible at one end. We'd have raspberries and potatoes from now on. The potato starters went in the bed by the tower.

Over time, we went all out and cleared the trees and brush downslope from the tower and brought back Mel's sea view. A worthwhile grunt.

WE HAD HEARD AND read about a floating garden experiment Meares Island way, so one day we set off to investigate.

left Bea at work in Mel's garden.

right Downslope, blooming vestiges from English settler days.

We'd been around the island before, once. Meares was half the size of Flores but far more convoluted, so on that initial recce we opted for the quickest route, avoiding the bays. The massive clear-cuts visible in the hinterland behind Meares only sped us along, and we got back to our starting point early, feeling a little glum. Many folks lived interesting lives back there—oyster-lease holders, artists in floathouses, happy hippies, and we had bombed past them. Inside waters felt eerie to us, a touch claustrophobic.

This time we didn't have to go far in; just around the corner of Catface and into Cypress Bay, a wide expanse partly claimed by a fish farm, and from there into Quait Bay, an enclosed harbour in the shape of an oak leaf. It held a resort featuring a handsome longhouse-like building and a floating structure. There was a classic tugboat at moorings, the *Ivanhoe*, and, to our astonishment, the McBarge from Vancouver's Expo 86.[1] The once shiny floating McDonald's restaurant now had a slimy, unkempt look. Why here? A gourmet palace awaiting a pressure wash? A floating horror film set?

Our main destination was nearby, a tiny cove behind a narrow channel. We nipped in. It was shaped like a womb and home to a most remarkable embryo—a compound made up of multiple floating platforms painted dark turquoise and magenta, hippie colours we recognized instantly from some splintered planks washed ashore on our beach after a winter storm. We'd wondered where they had come from.

We motored in slowly across still, dark waters pierced with shafts of olive light, passing a classic motor launch at mooring. Around us, forested hills descended to shore rocks frilled with algae.

Though arriving unannounced, we were greeted courteously by the couple in residence, Wayne and Catherine, people roughly our age.

With quiet pride they showed us around their garden crops in containers and greenhouses. There was fresh water from a stream, power from sun and generator, heat from wood stoves. There were several buildings, the largest their wooden home. To our surprise, they invited us in.

"We keep an open house in the summer," Catherine explained. Resort guests would paddle over from Quait Bay to buy their art.

They were both sculptors, and showed us intricate, delightful things they had made, he a walking stick, she a small owl. They worked wood, whalebone, and ivory on occasion, when the source was legal.

They were handsome, fairly slight people, with an elfin quality. There was something "other" about them, as if they might have a secret ability to flash a new skin colour or live underwater without benefit of air. They spoke of nature guiding the artist's hand, of the healing power of potherbs, of the interconnectedness of things. She wrote poems and had a dance background, exercising at the ballet barre daily. There was a platform for that.

The two had inhabited that cove for nearly fifteen years, tethered to the land by cables. They had built everything around them, mostly from recycled sources. Fireweed, a plant of many virtues, had inspired their colour scheme.

Though it was confined, they called their home Freedom Cove.

A LOW tide at dawn meant Sometimes beach was fully exposed. Add to that a cloudless sky and a light breeze playing with mist eddying off the incoming tide—I just *had* to be there. To my surprise, Kate was out on the rock taking in the morning rays. She had come in with clients the previous evening. They were still in their tents at the north end, so she picked up her rod and, together, we scrambled across the rocks onto the firm sand of Sometimes beach.

Each time Kate came to Vargas, we'd learn more about our adopted daughter. We knew she was bold just by the way she looked the world in the eye. We also learned (mostly from others) that she frolicked in the rapids of Skookumchuck Narrows in her kayak and competed in Oregon's big surf competitions, where she beat the hotshot guys. She taught kayaking and guided as far afield as Southeast Asia and Chile, and if she had spare time in winter, she'd work ski patrol. I grimaced when I saw the list of certificates and qualifications on her card. She laughed. "I hope you won't hold that against me," she said.

The pastels of Catface gained definition as the sun rose above Meares Island. A school of salmon moved through with small telltale swirls on the surface. Soon we each had a couple of nice fish laid out on the rocks, watched by ravens, guarded by dogs.

Bea arrived with her camera.

Occasionally the sea parted and
we could almost walk to Burgess.

Low tide: the rock shelves
above Sometimes beach.

I'D BEEN PHOTOGRAPHING the knitted, diamond-shaped ripples that occurred where water met from opposing sides over the sandbar shallows. The tide was low, but not low enough that I could walk very far out toward Burgess. Heading to the north rocks instead, toward John fishing, I spotted something just as I stepped onto the first boulder. It was a bit of fabric protruding from the sand. I pulled on it and out came a funky little woman's shirt. I rinsed it out in the sea and scrambled up the rocks and over to Sometimes beach to check out the wide shelf of flat rock now visible, a low-tide wonder with its complex, rippled, and surf-gouged surfaces. Perhaps I could find one of those loose rocks with the Swiss-cheese holes right through them.

Surprise: Kate! I showed her my prize shirt and she said, "Oh, that's mine! I lost it last year!" She'd put it down as she stopped to draw a message on the sand.

At the end of Sometimes beach was a cave, mysterious, slippery with kelp, and dark but for the shaft of light at the end, where a pile of rocks opened up to a cleft at the forest's edge. Water must have spouted out of it mightily in rough weather.

There was a place like Sometimes beach on Flores, hard to access through a tricky channel but rich with surf-scoured sandstone shelves and a vast selection of holey rocks. We went there sometimes when weather permitted. There had been squatters there, their cabins dilapidated and surrounded with mint gone wild.

Of the magical places we could walk to on Vargas, Green Room was the most impressive. An open cave Dylan and his friend D.J. had discovered on an early scout, it was my secret place of pilgrimage, marked by a nurse log (a fallen tree) high across its entrance, bearing three perfectly aligned live trees. The access was forbidding—a gap between sheer rock faces so narrow one had to sidle along sideways to reach the chamber. Inside, the skylit, curved walls dripped green with moss and maidenhair fern sparkling with moisture. On the ground, to the side, a mound of rocks, and beyond this, the entrance to a small, dank enclosure one could crouch into by lifting a lush curtain of moss strands. It was dark inside, spooky without a headlamp.

I took our friend Hana there once, with three others. She conducted a lighthearted rebirthing ceremony, being an expert in such

Precious remnants, from
jingle shells to holey rocks.

things. Each friend, in turn, entered the black chamber and soon
re-emerged fresh to the world and a little giddy. I didn't tell them
about the finger-length, ghost-white crickets hanging from the
cave roof.

More than likely, the Green Room, like the cave at Sometimes
beach, had once served as a place of send-off and spirit release—
but perhaps that too implied rebirth.

AMONG OTHER experts we got to meet or renew acquaintances with that year—including a bear expert and a bee expert—were the Primitives, a group of experienced outdoors folk who teach ancient skills. They converged on our beach from Oregon, California, and BC with our friend Martin. The surf was too crazy for Marcel to get them ashore on our beach, though Dylan, who'd come in the same boat, distinguished himself by jumping overboard carrying a desktop computer high above his head with waves up to his chest. The rest of the group went to Mel's beach to offload enough baggage for a small military operation. As surf battered the skiff, they struggled to land the boxes and bins. Many fell into the sea and had to be retrieved from along the beach.

For a week, they camped in front of our house in a canvas outfitter's tent complete with a miniature wood stove and camp beds. We'd sit on logs around their campfire while they whittled, flint-knapped, and hand stitched raw leather garments as they yarned. Goode, a blue-eyed Cherokee, found the shards of a Japanese glass ball on the rocks and while we watched, he knapped a perfect arrowhead as a house gift that Bea hung in the sunroom window. From Martin she received a pendant in the shape of a traditional halibut hook. Martin was a silversmith, a goldsmith—an alchemist—as well as a guide. Wes had his specialties in scrimshaw and music.

Sea glass: a collection.

The men dived, they fished. They went into the forest with Dylan, searching for perfectly shaped aged yew from which they made traditional longbows. Then they shaped arrows and spent hours plonking them into beach targets. I had always been uneasy about the male bonding thing, but by the time the Primitives left, we felt at one with their tribe.

IN JAPAN AGAIN: East coast of Hokkaido, Shiretoko Peninsula. July 1, we left the town of Rausu and drove north along the coast in a small convoy of four-by-fours loaded with bright-coloured kayaks and stuffed with people sitting on piles of gear. As the road narrowed, so the hillside to our left grew steeper, and the shore rockier. To the right, forty kilometres across the strait, Kunashiri, the first of the Kuril Islands, cut a rugged profile on the horizon.

"So that's Russia?" I asked, by way of confirmation. My driver snorted.

"Kunashiri belong Japan," he said, grimly. "Russia steal. Some day we take back."

The road narrowed further and eventually became impassable. At a seasonal fish camp, tucked behind a sturdy breakwater, a crop of orange tents had already been pitched on a boulder beach. Takehiro was there to greet me. It was good to see him again. He looked fit and strong, had put on some weight, and now that he was forty, sported a samurai tuft on the top of his balding head.

"It's a big group," he said apologetically. "Forty people."

"Forty in one group!" I gulped.

In North America, groups larger than twelve are considered unmanageable.

Take shrugged.

"It is Japanese way. You will see. It will be okay."

"Where's Shinya-san?" I asked.

"He will be here soon. He is repairing a kayak. We had last-minute sign ups."

I glanced over the boats on the beach, most of them somewhat vintage and heavily patched. One double had the rudder taped to its stern, clearly not intended for use.

"Shinya doesn't care too much about equipment," said Take, reading my thoughts, "but don't worry. He knows."

It was after dark when Shinya-san arrived with the last of the boats, an impressively patched double. The crowd around the campfire parted deferentially and one of his lieutenants ladled out a bowl of noodle soup for him from a large pot on the fire. He offered the bowl with both hands and a slight bow of the head. Shinya-san, a stocky, powerful man and one-time Himalayan mountaineer who looked more Inuit than Japanese, took the bowl with a nod and beamed. This was his world. He was supremely comfortable, surrounded by friends and loyal disciples.

We set off early next morning; a sea serpent of over thirty kay-aks off a wild and rugged shore much like the one I had just left. Shinya-san set a gentle pace with his lieutenants stationed along the snake, monitoring novices, ensuring no one strayed. Winds were light, skies clear, picture-perfect. Cormorants flapped heav-ily across the water as we made our way through rock gardens where a languid surge played "swish" with beds of kelp.

We stopped for lunch and climbed a steep bank of volcanic rub-ble overlaid with lilies and wild parsnip. A bleached Shinto shrine,

Shiretoko adventure: a lesson in
leadership, forbearance, thinking
big, and thinking on one's feet.

gateway to the wilderness, stood several hundred feet above the beach, on a flat shoulder of grassland grazed by a herd of Sitka deer. The cone of Mount Shiretoko loomed above us like a huge theatre prop, a wisp of steam rising from its summit. Shinya-san had brought a can of red paint and people took turns slapping the paint on the supporting posts of the torii gate and repairing the foundation to withstand another winter.

The torii gate commemorated the fate of the crew of a torpedoed Japanese merchant ship run aground at that point during the last winter of the Second World War. Those who managed to get ashore faced a grim fate as hypothermia and starvation picked them off. Only the captain and one crewman made it out to civilization by walking on the compacted ice floes.

A ceremonial cloth was laid on the grass, then green tea was brewed and passed around in delicate china cups. Everyone bowed twice, clapped twice, then bowed again to the elegant structure before we resumed our journey.

The Shiretoko Peninsula is the northeast corner of the Japanese archipelago, jutting out into the Sea of Okhotsk. Shiretoko means "the end of the Earth." Nobody lived on this stretch of the coast, now a National Park, though signs of human activity abounded in the form of empty fish camps and set nets anchored to the shore. We camped that first night at a sandy cove with an abandoned shack. There I found the motherlode of glass balls where discarded nets had rotted over the decades, leaving their floats part buried in long grass. Some amber coloured balls were clearly very old and bore distinctive manufacturer's marks. This explained why we could occasionally find such ancient glass balls on beaches in BC. All it would take would be an extra high tide or rogue wave to get them floating again. We were almost at the same latitude; neighbours across the ocean and the dateline. (Bea was seventeen hours behind me, probably dreaming about glass balls.)

Conditions smiled on our group as, over the next three days, we rounded the tip of the peninsula and headed south again toward the town of Utoro. One day, we paused for lunch beside a river of steaming hot water, then made camp near another where pink salmon spawned. Wildlife, particularly seabirds, hawks, and white-shouldered sea eagles, grew more plentiful. Herds of deer grazed the green shoulder between the sea and the forested slopes of Shiretoko, and then there were the Ussuri brown bears, dozens of them, as big and mean as grizzlies.

At the end of our second-to-last day, we arrived at the beach on which Shinya-san had planned to camp that night. A large Ussuri was foraging in the middle of it. Our armada hovered offshore while Shinya conferred with his lieutenants. Next, Shinya was ashore and approaching the bear, shaking a rock inside a pot, his can of pepper spray at the ready. But the bruin just continued turning over rocks and snuffling about for crabs. Shinya yelled, rattled his pot, and waved his arms. No response.

The Master returned to the group.

"Bear not move," he explained. "We camp further on."

So instead of a protected beach, Shinya and his staff landed on large, rounded boulders well beyond where the bear continued its nonchalant pursuit. Then, one by one, they guided the novice kayakers ashore, sliding their boats up the boulders so they could step out dry. Now I understood the patches on Shinya's boats.

During the night, the wind picked up. Surf crashed onto the boulders and in the morning, we were faced with large dumping breakers. There was no way I would have considered launching a novice group through such conditions and when I realized it was Shinya's intention to do so, I took Take aside and as tactfully as I could, suggested we carry the boats along the boulders to the now bear free beach.

Take frowned.

"Shinya knows," he said, holding up his hands to slow me down. "Shinya knows."

I said nothing more.

Shinya-san had seven lieutenants on this trip. They all put on their dry suits, and when everyone had their boats loaded at the water's edge, the team formed a human chain out into the surf, the sturdiest among them balanced further out on the slippery boulders. One by one, they slid the fully loaded boats, kayakers seated, over the boulders then fired them out between sets.

It was brilliant, and when the last participant was safely beyond the break, the staff helped me and one another launch till only Shinya remained. He picked his moment and launched languidly through the dumpers, then, cigarette hanging from the corner of his mouth, he took his place at the head of the procession.

The last day took us past towering vertical cliffs from which sea birds swarmed at our approach. It was the most exposed part of the trip with few chances to land all day. Tour boats from Utoro reached this far north loaded with tourists in city clothes. The seas here were home to more than a dozen species of cetaceans, with whale-watching as much a draw as it was at home. Orcas were common. There had been a mass stranding there two years before.

By the time we reached town, I was starting to think about my bed on Vargas. But we still had the symposium the next day, in Rausu. We loaded the boats onto waiting vehicles and drove across the peninsula to the bed and breakfast we had used as a base.

Take seemed worried as he strategized with his friend Taka, the outdoor gear rep who was co-sponsoring the symposium.

"Tomorrow very important," he said to me when their discussions seemed to have reached some sort of conclusion. "Some people want to stop kayakers visiting Shiretoko. It is a big land use issue. Tomorrow we have people from Ministry of Environment, National Parks, Forestry, Department of Fishing, also local politicians. Very important."

I nodded, starting to wonder where this was going.

"What do you want me to do?" I asked.

"You keynote speaker," he said solemnly, adding hastily, when he saw the alarm on my face, "Only one hour and half."

"An hour and a half!" I shrieked, "What do you expect me to say?"

Take smiled confidently.

"You will know what to say," he said.

Next day, as people were filing into the auditorium at the Rausu community centre, I insisted on a meeting with the organizers.

"So, what *am* I expected to say?" I demanded.

"Give your impressions of Shiretoko," Take said.

"For an hour and a half…?"

"Only three-quarter hour," Take corrected. "There will be translation." Everyone nodded agreement.

"Tell them what you think the park needs," said Taka.

"What it needs is a whole lot less commercial fishing presence if it is to be taken seriously as a World Heritage wilderness site," I said. "How can it be a wilderness park if you cross land-based set nets every kilometre? There should be no commercial fishing within three kilometres of the shore."

Panic crossed their faces.

"You cannot say that here," said Take. "If you say that we will have to leave town very fast. This is the centre of the fishing industry. They are very powerful."

"He can say it," said Taka. "He is a foreigner. He can say it."

About 150 people sat on folding chairs in the auditorium. Before a display of traditional baidarka kayaks sat a panel of dignitaries and specialists. I was surprised to see one of Shinya's lieutenants seated there. With his shaved head and coarse woollen clothing, I had assumed he was part of the team because he was a tough, competent, skilled paddler. Certainly he was always at hand when some task needed doing. It turned out he was also a distinguished scientist with a doctorate in environmental sciences, and he was the main technical speaker.

The Japanese people tend to give a lot of slack to foreign guest speakers. They even laughed at some of my jokes. Then came the serious business.

"Now I want to speak about the elephant in the room," I said.

Take, who was translating, looked at me like I had gone mad.

"Elephant in room?" he asked.

"Elephant in the room," I said. "The big thing that nobody mentions."

"Ahh!" said Take.

There followed a protracted explanation and I launched into my tirade against the overbearing presence of the commercial fishery and the plague of broken nets and garbage they had caused on the beaches of Shiretoko. Dan would have been proud of me.

"It is like where I come from," I said. "In Clayoquot Sound, we have fish farms and logging of old-growth forest."

Heads nodded in understanding but there were some hard stony faces. I sensed Take had chickened out and was filtering the message.

A panel discussion on land use followed my talk, and after that, a break for lunch. I found myself chatting with a young woman in a National Park warden uniform. She had done her PhD at Cambridge.

"Thank you," she said in impeccable English. "Your observations were the same as the UNESCO panel of scientists who reviewed our application for World Heritage status."

"It is all rather obvious," I pointed out.

Peeved again.

She smiled.

"Your translator did not really do justice to the bit about the elephant." Then she added, "The tradition of fishing this coast is a very difficult issue. Somebody from outside has to say it."

Bea, meanwhile:

JULY HAD BEEN BUSY, with the beach its usual happy parade. I was pleased with two of my little projects, one involving vacated crab shells collected in seven different sizes to represent the Dungeness shedding habit, the other involving empty sea urchin shells similarly arranged by size. These I had threaded onto an upward curving stick to hang on the wall. Nature provides.

It provides in surprising ways, sometimes, and at exactly the right moment. John was due back from Japan that afternoon and I hadn't been fishing. Guilt. But here is what happened: the eagle was at the water's edge, fighting with a flapping salmon. I said to Lolita, loudly, "Squeaky! Squeaky!" I followed as she rushed down to the beach to scare the eagle away. The eagle dropped the fish right by the shore. I picked it up and here we had it, the homecomer's dinner.

I had not found a glass ball this time. No matter. As I watched John unpack on his return, I noticed his socks and pantlegs were stuffed with glass floats from Japan. This had reportedly caused some consternation at Customs.

THE POND we'd dug the previous fall was on the edge of the skunk cabbage swamp behind the house, so it filled naturally. Water lily rhizomes from Monks Lake produced three robust round leaves in the spring, then to our delight, in midsummer, a bud broke surface and yielded a perfect yellow bloom. Red-legged frogs found their way to the new neighbourhood to lay eggs, followed closely by a family of garter snakes. A small, grey-footed duck came to visit on its way south. A female American wigeon, we figured. For two days it rested, feeding on seeds from rushes.

We'd placed bog cranberry and scavenged wild violets in clumps at the edge of the pond along with tiny irises Bea "rescued" from the beach. Unfortunately, the irises made for another Stinky Bob moment—the cute miniatures were in fact struggling yellow flag, an invasive species that shot to shoulder height when their roots found the moisture and rich soil they craved. Bea, in the end, wasn't displeased with her yellow flag experiment,

Pond visitors: a red-legged frog and blue-legged wigeon.

having discovered its fleur-de-lys connection and found some well-established specimens at the edge of the woods on Fingers. They were like us, in a way—trespassers who had worked hard for their residence privilege.

When Olympia saw our pond, she declared it in need of a Japanese maple, so next visit she arrived with an elegant, weeping specimen with dark red foliage. We added goldfish, then water snails, and the scene was complete. Next projects: a pond at Mel's place, then a new privy with a panoramic view and, eventually, a magical self-flushing feature (triggered by heavy rain) beyond the workshop.

"It's got splash-back," Marlin had once complained.

HIKERS RETURNING from Little Baja one morning mentioned meeting Louisiana Joe with a party of friends working on the trail.

Odd they hadn't stopped by, I thought; better go introduce myself.

I found three men and a woman hacking salal partway across the peninsula trail.

"Hi. Building a road?" I asked.

Suspicion flashed across their faces, gradually easing as I explained who I was and where we lived. Joseph, as he introduced himself, was a youthful sixtyish man with rapid-fire chatter, and his brand-new second wife, Natasha, was an athletic blonde from Belarus. Joe had hired Paul, a local hippie, to guide and do the

Bowing before the wind.

heavy hacking; the third man was a genial friend of Joe's along for the adventure.

I checked my watch.

"Why don't you join us for lunch," I said, adding, "Neighbours are few and far between around here."

We shared fresh salmon, salad, and cold beer. By the time the water taxi came to pick them up, we'd heard the story of Joe and Natasha's Internet-sparked romance and the reason for a puzzling marking on our chart, showing an underwater power cable running from Port Gillam to Joe's property line. Some trade he'd made way back in the day when cabling electricity seemed the smart thing to do. Like the winch, left waiting for the next stage.

As they were leaving, Joe gave us his business card and a tight roll of hundred-dollar bills. Protest was futile.

"Just keep an eye on my place," he said. "I don't want people cutting trees or squatting on the property."

AT THE end of summer, Olympia took leave of her job with her Tofino family, who by then had become firm family friends to us all. She had decided on a reset.

"I need to deal with my old fear of being alone," she announced.

She set a tent up near the middle of the beach.

"Take Bungie," I suggested.

"No. I wouldn't be alone then."

After a few days there, she moved to an islet at the western end of Louisiana Joe's land, connected to the shore by a log-jam and a ridge of sand between two pocket beaches. Near the extreme tip of the islet she had discovered a discreet opening, like a cave, a magical place beneath wind-sculpted trees. In the middle grew a lone chanterelle. This was to be her secret retreat.

The location was about as wild as you could get on Vargas, and a discovery for us. The little island shook each time a swell exploded at her doorstep. She anchored her tent as solidly as she could, then set up a ring of stones for her fire. Rice, oil, flour, tea, a pot and pan, a machete, a journal, and a pile of books were pretty much all she took. We helped clear a path across the middle of the islet so she could leave without having to scramble across slippery rocks or during high tide.

The girl already knew where to find wild onions and mushrooms. She collected razor clams from Little Baja, and mussels and barnacles from the rocks. She also had a fishing rod for kelpies. Wisely, she kept her kitchen well clear of her tent, on the beach at the opposite side of her island. Food was hung high, beyond wolf's reach. She did, however, leave her dishes and wash-up facilities down low. As a result, one morning she found a wolf had chewed a hole in her dishwashing liquid and drunk it all.

Our free-spirited offspring wore rock climbing shoes and not much else as the last summer days gave a final burst of warmth. There was a rumour among late-season hikers of a half-naked nymph with a machete who could run across rocks as fast as they could on hard sand, then just disappear.

When the first winter storm came, she moved into Mel's guest cabin, which she set up comfortably with enough firewood for winter and spring.

November and December saw dramatic winter light, and fresh moss in the forest glowed like emeralds in the filtered sun. Hard to imagine a more perfect place or time for a contemplative journey.

Not long before Christmas, our old friend Carlton John turned up from Queensland with Jenny, his new mate, who was amazed and delighted to be able to walk the forest paths without resorting to snake-proof boots. The BC cold was a shock, though, and they were soon quite ready to return to Cairns for barefoot life on their sailboat—but not before John had made some useful rigging improvements to *Tink*.

The cold snap resulted in surprisingly long hoarfrost forming on beach logs and a blanket of snow that stayed on the ground for weeks. The usual crowd was there for Christmas, cozy with the wood stove cranked high.

A Christmas wrapped in hoarfrost,
snow, and molten light.

Sweet abundance, new beginnings.

6

FLOTSAM, GUESSING GAME, AND A SET OF WHEELS

WE DIDN'T KNOW IT then, but those were the middle years, con-joined in our memory like two sides of a sandwich held together by its contents; or perhaps more like a teeter-totter resting on its point of balance, 2008 and 2009 bearing equal parts discovery and fulfillment, growth and consolidation. Until it so happened that we were catapulted forward to a bold new phase in our coastal experiment, inspired by a "boatmobile."

Surprise offerings

Just before Easter 2008, an industrial-sized plastic water tank came rolling across the waves toward Olympia on Mel's beach, driven by a northwesterly wind and borne on an incoming tide. It was exactly what we needed. I towed it around to our beach and the three of us rolled it into position behind the workshop where it could col-lect rainwater from the roof and connect to another tide-borne treasure—a length of specialized water line, likely from a fish farm.

Later that spring, Bea took some time away in Victoria, then in Vancouver—her first time back in four years. She hadn't missed the big city, but still it was a chance to visit with a newly rebooted "Miss Olympia," ballet repertoire teacher, and meet her friendly family of roommates living in a nice old home near city hall. This reminded Bea of her own youth. She came back all smiles, and in

After the hens' winter break we were short one egg and there was a spell of random sizing.

time to help me clean up a big mess on the south rocks, where fresh booty had washed up courtesy of the aquaculture trade: a floating dock made of pressed steel decking on a base of foam blocks, now stuck on a sloping cleft between the two beaches. Wave action had broken the polystyrene into millions of small pieces, but the steel remained to be cut up for projects such as fire grills and workshop flooring. (As we had for the waterline tubing, we'd asked around town to see who might reclaim it or tow it out as salvage. Not worth it, Marcel had said. Treasure to us nonetheless.)

The sea provided surprises of another kind.

As occurred once as I was jigging for bottom fish near BB Rock. That feels different, I said to myself, winding in my line. Up came a really angry pigeon guillemot, all tangled in line but not hooked. These birds can dive to huge depths. As I was carefully separating the mess of nylon and feathers, my catch looked me squarely in the eye, leaned its head back, and pecked the back of my hand really hard, drawing a single drop of blood. I cast the appropriate aspersions on its pedigree, finished disentangling it, and put it back in the water where it promptly dived. (Peculiarly, that tiny wound took five years to heal.)

Another surprise awaited related to the dogfish Alain hooked and brought aboard. Dogfish and inflatable boats make poor companions owing to the dogfish's nasty dorsal spines. Ideally, dogfish should be dropped back over the side and never brought aboard, but in this instance the hook was in deep. A few whacks with "the priest" (he who delivers the last rites), also known as a fish bat, and we headed home.

Dogfish is good eating if you skin it quickly and it was our only fish that day. Imagine our amazement to see our dead dogfish displaying what looked like acute symptoms of indigestion by the time we reached the beach. Something was banging and punching to get out. I slit open its belly and seven young dogfish emerged into the world. We dropped them in the sea and watched them swim off on the next stage of their adventure. The triumph of youth.

In summer 2009, exotic creatures were brought to our beach by El Niño. The first to wash ashore was a sunfish the size of a dinner table and just about as flat. The two large fins and tiny puckered mouth seemed out of character for a fish that weighed a tonne. Apparently, sunfish feed on by-the-wind sailors, which made sense since, given their cartoonish shape, catching anything else

might seem improbable. This one had been dead for some days and already the skin, tough like medieval armour, was showing signs of loosening. Once they got the available eye, the scavengers could do nothing further with it, leaving its fate to the tide.

Next to reach us were juvenile Humboldt squid. These came ashore by the hundreds, gasping and writhing beside those that preceded them. Apparently carried north by the warm current then encountering cold water off Vancouver Island, they suffered a systems shutdown. Most were about a metre long, each a calamari feast. We loaded a wheelbarrow with the freshest, stripping out the thick white meat for eating as ceviche, or flash frying in oil infused with herbs and garlic. We weren't the only scavengers out there—also eating their fill were eagles, ravens, gulls, crows, and wolves. It was a feast for the taking.

Bea even collected their sharp black "parrot" beaks for one of her more ghoulish projects.

Yet another sign of El Niño was the arrival of a tree loaded with thousands of pelagic gooseneck barnacles. We pondered their edibility and decided against it. They drooped flaccidly off the branches like so many tiny pink penises.

(One earlier year, I had found a more appealing menu item, locally sourced, as I motored down Calmus Passage—a drowned deer, still quite fresh. I cut short my errand and rushed back home to dress it. Good meat. The animal must have taken to the water to escape a wolf or cougar and the plan backfired.)

Pelagic gooseneck barnacles on the sands of Little Baja after a long, log-borne journey.

A regular at the reading nook.

Books of revelation

THERE WAS A NEW title out by Margaret Horsfield, the author of *Cougar Annie's Garden*: *Voices from the Sound—Chronicles of Clayoquot Sound and Tofino 1899–1929*.

I was thrilled: Here was a fat book with that rare mixture of wit and minutiae, full of great yarns about Indigenous Peoples, shopkeepers, settlers, sealers, prospectors, and small-boat heroics. I zeroed in on the Vargas bits. But what drew my attention the most were photographs from the first decades of the Christie Indian Residential School—images of girls at their tasks, neat in matching dresses and aprons, of boys in uniforms holding band instruments; of nuns, priests, a handsome white building surrounded by stumps, then gardens; of canoes and picnics—yet the faces made the blood run cold, so hauntingly sombre were they.

The Catholic institution had been created there in 1900, as a bulwark against an increasing Protestant presence on the coast.

Whatever other memories remained of the long-lived school, its early principals and priests live on as names on the map: Brabant Channel, Father Charles Channel, Father Charles Rock, Moser Point, Maurus Channel… and our own Calmus Passage, named after Father Ildephonse Calmus, a man inordinately fond of corporal punishment.

Kakawis, the site's original name, means "place of berries."

Same year, another book: the album-sized *Builders of the Pacific Coast*, a treasure trove showing traditional Indigenous construction methods and the work of almost fifty contemporary builders dotted along the coast from Northern California to Vancouver Island. Among them were people we knew or knew of, like Lloyd the Catface architect, Wayne who built the log-framed lodge at Quait Bay, and a trio of clever Tofitians.

I almost choked on my tea biscuit when I came across them— photos of houses that looked exactly like ours, built by a pioneer surfer dude who was not Dick, but rather a Bruno. Cabin details were eerily similar down to the flooring made from upright rounds. Some were built for Cougar Annie's successor at Boat Basin, Hesquiaht Harbour; others were at remote marine sites. One, The Wreckage in Ucluelet, we'd seen but only from the outside. Bruno and Dick would have known each other, one working on the other's team, no doubt? We'd have to find out.

We sent a copy of this book to Louisiana Joe, who still dreamt of putting his winch to use to build something nice on his view spot. Some months later he sent photos of what he had in mind—the sparse yet sumptuous structure of a Japanese garden temple, with balconies on four sides. Could we help tackle such a project for him? Paul had plans ready. Joe would be visiting before too long and let us in on the details.

The next set of news was that Natasha was pregnant and Joe would become a father at sixty-seven. There was no chance of another trip for a while. In fact, he was listing his land with an agent, keen to organize his affairs in view of the increased family responsibilities.

So from then on, although we saw him again and stayed in touch, it was mostly his selling agent we were in contact with.

We worked on his paths a little bit each trip to Fingers and beyond.

Just guessing

May through September, we had been meeting so many people that I took to playing a guessing game, mostly by myself, but on occasion openly. One evening, I was walking Mel's beach looking for salmon "jumpers" when I came across five new arrivals, middle-aged guys with all the right gear, sitting around a campfire sipping wine from enamel cups. It looked like an expensive bottle. Five top-end kayaks were pulled up on logs. Lolita had already gone ahead to check out the food situation. I looked them over, then said with exaggerated thoughtfulness, "Emergency room physicians."

The view from Louisiana Joe's house site.

They nearly fell off their logs.

"Not quite," one replied. "He's a psychiatrist. Keeps us sane."

The offending outsider nodded in acknowledgement.

"Dammit," one said, "are we that obvious?"

They all worked at the hospital in Canmore, Alberta, and this was their annual escape into anonymity. They handed me a cup of wine and I squatted beside their fire. It was the start of a nice friendship.

Next day, they dropped by for lunch, then, in the afternoon, news came through that one man's toddler had been rushed to hospital in critical condition. Bless those smartphones. I scrambled the father to Tofino in the inflatable so he could charter a plane out that evening. We stored his kayak and gear till a friend could pick it up. Happily, his child recovered, and we received a very fine bottle of wine when the friend came.

Sometimes I got it spectacularly wrong. I figured the woman with the shaved head and black track suit was some kind of police instructor or maybe military, a ninja on a weekend off. Her partner had a Quebec accent and a similarly shaved head. I reported back to Bea and that evening we went down to cast for coho off the beach. The Ninja and the Frenchie came to watch us haul salmon ashore and introduced themselves, Patti and Yves. She worked for the Victoria school board and he with the Francophone Cultural Centre in Victoria. On the side, the two taught private sea kayak classes. The shaved heads were a celebration of summer freedom. Much chatter ensued in two languages.

Not long after this, a woman knocked at the door to ask if the mussels were safe to eat, a fair question due to occasional red tide closures. Bea, who was inside, heard the voice. She came out and stared at the woman's face.

South rocks with Hobbs
and Burgess Islets.

In 2009, there was a new net to try out to catch needlefish. It worked.

opposite At the end of April, end of May, early June, and on the solstice, the tide was low enough for a morning's fishing at Sometimes beach. In April, there was sun and cloud; in May, it was grey; and in June, there was fog. But always, there were salmon, or at least needlefish enough for a pan of fritters. And always, there was gratitude for the privileged access we had to such a place.

"Myriam?" she asked.

"Beatrice!"

They flew into each other's arms. Myriam had been a colleague at *Business in Vancouver*, and they had lost touch when we left for Europe.

Sometimes there was no guessing involved; just a need to listen, to ask a question or two, and let things unfold. So it was once, when I was walking back from fishing at the north rocks. A lone kayaker had pulled ashore. I helped drag his boat clear of the waves. He was a big-boned guy about my age and seemed to know what he was doing.

"So, what brings you to these parts?" I asked.

"I just needed space to think," he said. Then out it came. "A competitor wants to buy my company and I don't know if I should sell." He looked along the beach as if seeking clarity. "My son wants me to go into business with him building specialty aircraft parts." All this while we were still standing at the water's edge.

I picked up the bow of his boat and we started up the beach.

"Would you want to do that?" I asked, trying to imagine what it would be like building aircraft parts with Dylan.

"Yes. I would like that," he replied.

"Was it a fair offer?"

"It was a good offer."

We put the kayak down above the high tide line.

"I reckon you have your answer," I said.

He stood there a little dazed, arms streaked with drying salt.

"I reckon so," he said. "That was easy."

He had already left when we walked by the next morning.

Assorted pursuits

For some time, I'd been tempted to trot out the paints. There was a market for local art at Tofino galleries and tourist shops.

Action. To Bea's horror I set up a production line, painting with oils on cedar shakes. I would line up twenty shakes with the centres sanded smooth, then move along the line painting the same feature on each one—mostly the tall dead cedar (Bea's "beseeching tree") or the porch view of the Shot Islets and Flores around sunset. In a couple of hours, I could produce twenty tourist-ready pieces of junk art that sold for seventy-five dollars apiece.

"Don't even think about signing them," Bea warned.

Eventually I moved on to watercolours, which had been my passion, off and on, for years. Progress with technique always came in fits and starts for me. This time the big leap was when I figured out how to paint quickly with wet paper. No Toni Onley here, but the pieces were a notable improvement on anything I had done before, so long as I resisted the urge to tweak the final product. I loved the freedom that came from working fast, sometimes completing several paintings in a morning. Often, I was so engrossed in what I was doing I'd lose track of time and the fact that I hadn't eaten. After a month, I had dozens of paintings ready to mount, then, during a visit to Vancouver, I bought framing materials and a mat cutting device. A local gallery carried them for an absurdly high price . . . and most sold.

My subjects came from the surrounding beauty—sea, sky, beaches, trees, particularly the two big cedars behind the house. I was drawn to wild stormy skies and misty coastal scenes. So amazed was I by the contrasts between sea and sky that I took to photographing seascapes in different light to confirm that the sea could indeed be dark purple when the sky was light grey with a blush of apricot, while the same scene could be a milky green sea with sullen grey cloud just a short time later.

Bea, meanwhile, worked on driftwood, bone, and dried kelp creations. She spent hours crouched over the bench in the workshop, enhancing natural lines, adding features, or just looking at them to see where they wanted to go. Eventually she set up her own studio in the Appendix, painting with acrylics on wood.

Nature's brush: life imitating art.

It was a creative flare-up that had been smouldering ever since we arrived on the island. For me, the flame burned brightly for a few months, then it dimmed. I had emptied my reservoir. Bea, as was her nature, worked steadily and thoroughly, taking weeks to complete a single piece. Meanwhile, I moved on to building tables and chairs from burls and driftwood, but these mostly went as garden furniture or gifts to friends. It felt like we were doing the right kind of work for the place, beyond the caretaking.

Increasingly, it also felt like we had a useful role to play as beach dwellers and kayak observers. Spring and fall, we now knew, were for kayak training operations and school groups, while summer was for guided tours and private groups. Most commercial operations were safe and well organized, from Dan and Bonny's leadership courses to school parties and experiential learning programs like Outward Bound. There was, however, a problem group that came each year with about a dozen young teens. Their instructors were not much older than the students, with little training or on-water experience. One year, they needed rescuing when attempting the five-kilometre crossing of Brabant Channel to Whitesands Beach in open canoes. In June 2009, they'd made it to our beach as the weather broke.

The storm blew and rained hard for four days. The group had no tents and only a single tarp, which they rigged a few feet from the ground for everyone to crawl under at night. When we spoke on day two, their sleeping bags were sodden and they were standing around a smouldering fire shivering, watching their leader try and coax heat into some wet, charred wood. Water dripped off the students' hair onto black garbage bags substituting for raincoats, holes cut out for heads and arms. Some of the boys were grey with cold.

We took them back to the Appendix to dry out and warm up and later showed them how to rig a tarp properly and set the right sized fire beneath it. Our pile of lost-and-found raingear outfitted everyone with a set of waterproofs. After they left, I wrote a letter to their parent organization and, at Francis's request, sent a copy to BC Parks. (The following year, they arrived with tents, rain gear, and properly equipped boats. Their staff had received extra training.)

We performed another, more amusing intervention for a different group when two teenaged girls turned up at the cabin one morning pleading for toilet paper. They had gone AWOL and hiked over from Hidden beach with the distressing story of having left that vital item behind in Vancouver. They were followed closely by an apologetic teacher who herded them back to camp, but not before they had secured several rolls of precious booty.

Wheeling and dealing

Summer 2009, I discovered what sounded too good to be true—a New Zealand–built amphibious RIB. It could drive straight out of the water and up the beach and might well have been designed for where we lived. I wanted one. There was a catch, of course: they were expensive. As a believer in the axiom that where there is a will, there is a way, I contacted the manufacturer to see if they were looking for a dealer in Canada. I knew the only chance I could justify such a purchase (not to mention the truck and trailer required) to my good wife would be to cloak it as a business. Even that would be pushing it.

New Zealand had just appointed a Canadian distributor in Ontario, and they sent me the address along with a glossy brochure to drool over. An Ontario importer would need someone in BC, so I contacted Paul, the owner, suggesting he sell me a boat wholesale as a demo. My credentials in the industry were good with no bridges burned. We made a deal, and I took possession of a dazzling, white, magical craft that promised to do everything but fly. It did not disappoint.

The boat was built stronger than one supported throughout its length by water. Three wheels had to endure the weight of six people, an inboard engine for the hydraulics, and an outboard. Each rear wheel had its own hydraulic motor. Hydraulic rams raised and lowered the wheels at the flick of a toggle on the console. All this added weight, which meant the boat was heavy for its size, but the placement worked to its advantage in rough water. It could handle most inside chop in Calmus Passage without slowing down or taking water. I loved driving it. It was a whole new adventure. Bea was grumpy about the way I'd bought it but had to admit she preferred it to the little boat. It even had a Bimini top for some protection from rain. She was less enthusiastic about the vinyl garage tent I set up for it by the boathouse.

What, a boatmobile?

The extra length helped break out through surf. Well, actually it meant that surf that was out of the question in the little boat was now possible. And because it had a two-stroke outboard, a three-to four-metre break was worth a poke. As part of the "learning how far to push it" process, I took on one breaker that curled right over the bow *and* the stand-up console. It dumped squarely on top of my head as I stood at the wheel. The handmade felt hat Olympia had brought me from Australia wumped down over my eyes and the boat was awash. But all it took to empty it was a burst of speed and what water did not slosh over the transom was quickly taken care of by two large scuppers.

Paul was in Tofino to check out the area and make sure his new agent was legit. First on the list of where to show the boat was the Clayoquot Wilderness Resort, an all-inclusive glamping experience for the uber-wealthy at the head of Bedwell Sound, beyond Freedom Cove. There, a family of four could pay in the tens of thousands for a week in a pioneer-style canvas tent decked out with Persian rugs on a platform floor. (Two Hollywood stars had wed there the year before, the luscious Scarlett Johansson and no less luscious Ryan Reynolds, a Vancouver lad.)

The resort was at the end of a twenty-kilometre run down a narrow glacial fjord. Rock walls rose straight from deep dark waters to peaks that were snow clad much of the year. The only signs of human activity along the way were fish farms, tucked into coves like floating junkyards, and the occasional sport fishing boat speeding by on its way from the resort to open sea.

Styled after a dude ranch, the resort was built along grassy river flats that meandered inland.

We dropped the wheels and climbed a steep ramp to a cluster of rustic buildings and laid the boat down on the lawn in front of the restaurant. The astonished patrons left their eggs Benedict and cappuccinos and crowded around. The manager, who welcomed the diversion, offered Paul and me a tour of the property in an elderly SUV, taking us everywhere except the guest accommodations, where they had 100 percent occupancy. The recession, it seemed, did not affect their guests. Reassuring, since such people were our most likely customer base.

Up the valley, two black bears grazed with horses in a lush field. They did not look up as we drove by.

Preparing for a washdown.

"We don't bother them, and they don't bother us," our host explained, "but we do have strict rules about leaving food around tents."

We passed a habitat restoration project designed to bring back a coho salmon run decimated by generations of brutal logging practices. Hundreds of tiny fry could be seen flitting in the shadow of submerged logs. A series of horseback and hiking trails led far back to the Strathcona watershed. Then there was archery, kayaking, and care for younger children, with picnics on islands like Whaler, but no wheely boat. And no, they didn't want one.

Mr. Toad's Wild Ride

We had been friends with Victor since 1979, having met when he worked for a venture capital company and I was a "penniless" foreigner who had just received a permit to capture fifty-eight troublesome Sayward Valley elk and needed finances for an elk ranch. That exotic project gave us a certain cachet around their office. It was further enhanced by our arrival at his fortieth birthday potluck bash with a roadkill pie made from a young black bear struck and killed by a vehicle on the Cypress Bowl road. It was, we believe, the most popular dish at the table.

Victor brought his good wife and four friends to visit one blustery fall day. I picked them up in Tofino with my new boat and ran them to our beach on the inside. We ate lunch, shared a bottle of wine, and walked the beaches.

Before taking them back, I asked the assembled group if they wanted to go the same way or take the more challenging outside route. There was loud enthusiasm for the outside from the guys. I failed to notice the quiet doubts of one woman.

The crux was the La Croix group, that maze of rocks and swirling kelp at the southern end, where waves crashed in a particularly chaotic mess. Though I knew the route, it proved terrifying for our anxious boater, who could see no obvious way through.

She could barely speak by the time we reached Tofino. My mistake. I'd broken the cardinal rule of group travel—pay heed to the most risk-averse participant.

A local whale-watching boat out on a shakedown trip well before the season start.

Bea refers to this incident as "Mr. Toad's Wild Ride." Less dramatic adventures in the boatmobile included driving up onto the sandbar that appears at low tide in front of Tofino and to the town's Co-op gas bar to fill up.

Returning with
rockfish and cod.

A GARDEN LOST
AND FOUND

PEA-GREEN against its conifer surround, the garden we restored to the light and now tend to has three parts: a wild patch, shared with huckleberry and salal; a pond area, claimed by lily pads; and a kitchen garden, where crops grow in bins and rows. Flowers make up the in-between.

Toiling here is a joy, a feeling rekindled each year by the buzz and *chee-dit* of hummingbirds. We flit as they do, feasting on our surroundings.

IN THE WILD PATCH Two representa-
tives from Mel's island: self-heal and
nodding onion.

PONDSIDE Native irises, wild violets,
and clover from a seaside springbank.

KITCHEN GARDEN

Queen rhubarb shares its space with annual crops: garlic or potato, peas climbing the fish nets. (Also in use, logboom chains found on the big beaches, still attached to drift logs.)

Herbs and salad greens occupy the chest-high roller-top planter boxes (unseen behind the chicken coop), root vegetables the others.

Like the carrots, many crops yield enough for copious reserves or preserves. (Our favourite preserve remains one from the wild: red huckle-berry jelly, ruby in a jar.)

COTTAGE GARDEN BLOOMS Some contribute nectar, others the colour and crunch for our salads (daylilies, borage, nasturtiums).

above, left Trim at her jungle gym, the gateway to the outhouse at the northern end of the garden. She is about to yowl for rescue.

The sun's shy stand
against darkness.

7

STARK CONTRASTS

IT WAS TO BE a year of contrast between lives marked and lives lost. By early spring, I had achieved senior and pensioner status and three of us had made plans to attend my mother's one hundredth birthday in May. Weeks before Bea, Olympia, and I headed to New Zealand for the grand celebration, Trim the cat became ill. Vet visits and medication brought little relief. Her chest had a crinkly sound, and she had a strange little cough, attributed to heart worm or some tropical ailment she may have long harboured. We knew by our departure day that we wouldn't see her again. Alain was left in charge of house and pets and given the sad task of caring for her. Trim had already decided it was time to die, it seemed, and spent the days on her favourite cushion near the stove, drinking little, and refusing food. The dogs seemed to understand and lay close. Like a Buddha, she graciously accepted everyone's love and attention. We said our goodbyes and thank yous for a good shared life.

It was the first time Bea and I had left the beach together for more than an overnighter, so she prepared a "House Notes" booklet for Alain and any future house-sitters. It surprised us how much detail there was to cover. Our simple island life was, in fact, complicated. Between "House cookstove" and "Emergency numbers/Locking up the house," there were two dozen headings, with "Animals" and "Getting to high ground" the longest sections.

The Vancouver Boat Show that year had been pre-empted by the Olympics, but the Victoria show went ahead and, before we caught our flight, I dropped my fancy white boat off for Paul to

Sixty-fifth birthday bonfire.
Less than two months later,
in the same place, there
would be a pyre for Trim.

sell. I was sad to part with it, but once in Auckland, we visited the factory and discovered that the manufacturer had come out with a new all-wheel-drive model that could perform like a tractor on land, even climb over logs . . .

The birthday bash was held at the retirement village where my mother lived. A big crowd attended, songs were sung, there was a giant cake, a copper beech was planted in her honour, and she gave a thoughtful speech in a strong, clear voice that belied her diminutive size.

We came back to Alain, three living pets, and one small frozen body shrouded in our friend's green T-shirt, its edges tucked neatly and stapled to a cedar board, awaiting a pyre on the beach. It was a dignified send-off for Trim, and to her smouldering remains we added the handful of Cobber's bones Olympia and Dylan had discovered in the woods.

TWO STRANGE events followed, salvage operations both. One brought cash and levity, the other deep tragedy.

Alain and I had set off on the morning beach walk. To our astonishment, a large black barge had washed ashore at the north end, right near the rocks. It was about the size of an average house, a rusty, mussel-encrusted monster of heavy planks built on two large steel pontoons, each tapered at both ends like a gigantic river catamaran. At one end, a couple of box structures and a fuel drum gave it the appearance of a submarine from a distance. Against the grandeur of Catface Mountain, its presence was an offence.

We had heard about it on the news during the night but thought nothing more of it till there it was. Coast Guard radio described it as a barge for helicopter logging. It had broken free from a tug on its way from Winter Harbour to Ucluelet and was considered a hazard to navigation.

"It looks expensive," Alain said as we drew closer.

"Lucky it came ashore on clear sand. It would have been destroyed on the rocks."

"Might be salvage," Alain said.

Bea had been out taking photos in the early morning light, and caught up with us, clicking away.

"What an ugly beast," she said. "We'd better call the Coast Guard and let them know it's here." By "we" she meant me.

JANUARY 12, 2010, a catastrophic 7.0 earthquake shakes Haiti, sending ripples of horror across the world. An estimated 160,000 people die, and a small, beautiful country is brought to its knees once again. Exactly a month later, there is international jubilation in Vancouver over the opening of the Winter Olympics. Competitions are still in progress when an 8.8 magnitude earthquake strikes Chile, spawning tsunami warnings all along the Pacific coast.

Goodnight Whaler,
goodnight sun.

Expensive junk, up for salvage.

I went to the point for cell service and called the Coast Guard, and then the RCMP, and BC Parks for good measure.

As I was returning, a seaplane swooped low over the trees and circled tightly, faces pressed against the windows.

"We should get an anchor from the boat shed," I said. "If we are going to claim salvage, we need to have a line attached to this thing."

Alain and I trotted back to the house leaving Bea to guard the prize.

We set the first anchor with its attendant buoy out as far into the surf zone as we could reach without swimming, then returned for a second, larger one to set at an angle up the beach in case the increasing surf knocked the barge sideways onto the rocks before we could tow it out to sea. When we got back to the barge with our wheelbarrow full of rope and the second anchor (itself the subject of a prior salvage), a small white runabout was hovering off the surf zone facing off with Beatrice, who stood defiantly at the water's edge pointing at herself, then the barge, and mouthing, "Mine!"

"They tried to grab our buoy," she said.

As we watched, the boat, with three men aboard, made another attempt to scoop up the float in what by now was a hefty surf break and building with the rising tide. One of the men lunged for the float with a boat hook and was almost thrown into the water as a breaker smacked into the side, bringing the boat close to capsize. They barely escaped being swept ashore and managed to scuttle for open water, where they waited.

"That is our barge," one man yelled.

"It is salvage," I replied.

"There is a tug with a five-thousand-pound pull on its way," he yelled.

"Great," I yelled back.

The tug was one of the powerful aluminum workboats that pulled barges to fish farms. It had a crew of two and came alongside the white fishboat where the crews held an impromptu conference as they tried to decide what to do about the fierce grey-haired lady with the camera on the beach. I, meanwhile, returned to the boathouse and launched the inflatable.

The tide was halfway up the beach by the time I joined the other two boats beyond the surf line.

"You can't claim that as salvage!" the tugboat skipper, a crusty, bleary-eyed old fellow yelled across the water to me. He'd been up all night looking for the barge he'd lost and was very grumpy.

"I have," I said.

"I'll call the police."

"I did already, and Coast Guard and Parks too. They seemed real worried about oil spills."

"Oh man, this is going to be messy," the grumpy one said.

He spoke briefly to a well-dressed man who had appeared from below and was standing back listening.

"Okay, I'll tell you what. I'll pay you five hundred bucks cash to take our line ashore and make it fast to the barge."

I considered the offer for about half a second. I certainly did not want their junky old barge. For us, it was a game. For them, it was a big worry.

"Deal," I said. "But your guy must be the one to attach the line."

"No problem."

The skipper collected the cash from among the crew and passed it over. A seaman climbed into my boat and we ran a light line through the surf to shore. He then pulled a heavy nylon hawser from the tug and made it fast to the barge, which was by then partially afloat. Tension came on the line and the sea astern the tug frothed and seethed.

Another April day on Mel's island.

Bang!

I was glad their man ran with the hawser because the strut he attached it to gave way with a sound like a rifle shot and was catapulted into the sea. The line was retrieved, reattached, and power applied once again. This time it held. Slowly the barge moved and broke free. Out through the surf and on her way she went.

Alain was, as well as a photographer, a retired colonel in an elite navy unit. As we walked back to the house I asked, "Alain, was that salvage, or was it piracy?"

He gave a Gallic shrug, said "Bof," and smiled.

(I ran into the tug skipper at the boat show a year or two later and told him we'd donated the money to the Friends of Clayoquot Sound for their No Logging campaign. He laughed.)

Patches and stitches

The old inflatable had developed a major leak along the seam between the aluminum hull and the portside tube. It needed warranty repair in Vancouver and an engine change from a pull-start, four-stroke, to an electric-start, e-tech, two-stroke to spare my aging shoulder joint.

Normally this would not have been a problem since we had a new small trailer for the truck, but when I went to pick it up at the Fourth Street dock, all I found was a cut padlock beside the iron post it had been chained to.

The weather forecast looked good, so at noon I loaded extra fuel and a pack with clothes and sleeping bag into the boat and headed for the Strait of Juan de Fuca, drain plug open, water rushing in through the leaks and right out again.

A light westerly breeze ruffled a following swell. Huge beds of kelp reached out into the strait, a testament to the return of the sea otter. Sea otters eat sea urchins, which eat the base of kelp forests that provide the nursery for herring, that feed the salmon, that feed sea lions and orcas . . . and so on. Thank you, sea otters, not just pretty faces.

Processions of freighters, fishing boats, and naval vessels gave me a good sense of my own size—or lack thereof—as they passed to and from Vancouver and Tacoma.

AT THE END OF MAY, the remains of a crashed floatplane on a charter flight to Ahousaht are retrieved from the waters between us and McKay Island. In it are the bodies of four people in their prime.

Nitinat Lake, a long, narrow flooded valley with tidal access I had often wanted to visit, was inaccessible when I arrived: the tide was low with hard-to-predict breaking surf. Misadventure there would not have been pretty, given how remote and exposed it was. I saw no sign of other people. Nearby, sea lions prowled the kelp forests or lay sunning themselves on boulders, paying no attention to my little boat. At sea, pigeon guillemots and marbled murrelets dived in panic as I burst into their world. A cormorant eyed me anxiously till it lost its nerve and flopped off its rock, leaving a trail of diminishing rings across the water till flight was achieved.

The sun had set by the time I cruised into Victoria Harbour in search of a place to pull ashore and lay out my sleeping bag. It was not looking good till I spoke with a military couple sipping wine in the cockpit of their sailboat in a marina.

"You're welcome to sleep on the boat," the man said. "Just clip the padlock closed when you leave in the morning."

I did not have chart coverage for the next part of the journey and was relying instead on a tourist road map of Vancouver Island. It did not show the US border clearly. Next morning, as I cruised between some islands, I noticed the American flag fluttering from a freshly painted flagpole. I'd crossed into the US near Stuart Island, at a point where the border zigged as I zagged. Half expecting a chase boat or shots, I sped on, but Homeland Security was asleep, or perhaps someone figured I was just another dozy Canadian off course.

In Vancouver, I got the boat fixed and exchanged the four-stroke for the two-stroke. Back home, the new motor was a game changer since it required no warming up, and Bea did not need to stand five minutes holding the boat in the surf. It was also more powerful and cleaner running. Unfortunately, before I quite got the hang of locking and unlocking it down, I managed to drop the bracket onto my thumb. It could easily have sliced it off, but I was lucky and eight stitches from Pam at the local hospital did the trick.

Soon after that, Bea and I returned from a walk to Dunes to discover that the silk screen on the water barrel near the front door had suffered major trauma and was stitched together like Frankenstein's monster, or my thumb. A note left on the front door explained that an instructor we knew had knocked to say hi, backed up, and fallen into the water barrel. I built a handrail from a contorted yew branch soon after that.

Evacuation

We made a support arrangement with Outward Bound. They had temporarily contracted out their summer operation to the commercial school co-owned by our friend J.F. and staffed by Kate. We shuttled and stored their gear and food. I had worked at three of these schools in my youth so had an idea of what was required and was able to backstop for emergencies as well. On one occasion, I helped rush someone with a hyperventilating and anaphylactic reaction to a bee sting to Tofino hospital. On another, I evacuated an aggressive, disruptive student and put him on the bus home.

The courses seemed less hardcore than they had been in the old days. "No more early-morning swims and no more working toward a final unaccompanied expedition. And no risk," Dawson grumbled. On the other hand, they still did a solo bivouac camp on a beach with a wolf issue.

Our beach was now better appointed for kayak campers. In the early spring, a chopper had dropped off two sturdy metal food caches with lockable doors and two green, plastic, throne-style toilets. The old pits had been filled in and new ones dug by a squad of smartly uniformed BC Parks personnel.

Part of the Outward Bound program was to provide service to local communities, so we had them help us cut a tsunami escape route from the north end to a safe high point. We'd worried about groups getting caught on the beach, so took to telling everyone about this new evacuation route. At first, we'd put up a notice at the beginning of the path, but Francis had apologetically taken it down, explaining that BC Parks considered it a liability risk! We had also long fantasized about a path to Port Gillam—a way in or out in impossible weather, through Crown land. But that too had been scotched, for fear of attracting more casual, less committed visitors to the outer beaches.

Meanwhile, changes of a major nature were underway across the water on Flores. Trees had come down along the shoreline, and preparation had started on a new subdivision at Ahousaht.

The ever-changing colours
of Millar Channel.

A blur of migratory peeps, a murder
of crows, and a gull colony huddled
against November cold.

The family

Bea went to Vancouver to help paint Olympia's newly purchased condo. The roommates had dispersed when the old house was demolished. Olympia was now pregnant with the first of three children she would have with her new-found partner, Aron.

In November, my mother became ill with a treatable infection. She declined the antibiotics and by the time Dylan and I arrived, she was lying serenely in her bed, beyond speech. I knew she could hear us, though. I held her hand and read her favourite poems from a small book she kept beside her bed. Just to check, I said to Dylan in a chatty way that I thought real estate was a bad idea for some money he had saved. Mum grunted and struggled to speak. She had long been an advocate of real estate as an investment.

"That's okay mum," I said, "just pulling your leg."

She gave an audible sigh of relief. It was our last little joke.

She died that afternoon. A long peaceful exhale, then nothing. I marvelled that the process of breathing had continued without pause for over a hundred years. The long struggle was over. Dylan, her granddaughter Debbie, and I slept on the floor in her room that night. In the morning, they took her body to the funeral home.

As we left, we checked the copper beech planted in the garden in her honour. It was doing well.

Bea had her own health predicament that winter.

THERE WAS FAIRLY EXTENSIVE, strange bruising around my upper thighs. I showed Drs. Pam and John, who were puzzled and sent me to Tofino hospital for a thorough exam. "Where have you *been*?" the nurse asked. Doctor No. 3 was equally puzzled and looked up a few possibilities, some of which were dire. Lyme disease was mentioned. I was sent off to a specialist in Nanaimo. John put me on the bus. Dylan would intercept me over there and drive back with me.

The specialist was more pensive than puzzled, and asked many questions. Lifestyle came up. When I volunteered there was an outhouse in my everyday life, her face lit up.

"Cold panniculitis," she announced genially, index finger up. "I've seen this in some horse rider patients. It's from riding saddle in cold conditions."

The bruises went away soon after.

The new outhouse: not as pretty as the old one, with its moon-crescent cutout, but it had a view.

That was not the last of our outhouse mishaps. The "House Notes" from around that time said this:

WOLVES: Bring the dogs inside when there are wolves around. We find tracks on the beach at 2- to 3-week intervals. Carry bear bangers and bear spray, plus a big stick on hikes; most importantly, carry a whistle to call Lolita back if she takes off after wolves. Bea wears her whistle around her neck and carries bear bangers in her pocket even in the garden, as several encounters have taken place just in front of the house, first thing in the morning or at dusk. To our knowledge, there is a pack of four plus two loner wolves on the island. The male from the pack is black and very large; he has bitten Lolita twice. She will gladly avoid confronting him if you blow the whistle.

It turns out there were four or five juveniles around on the occasion Bea visited the outhouse in the midnight hours.

Hearing yells, I rushed downstairs with my noisemaker of choice, the shotgun. Wolves everywhere.

I fired into the air. *Boom!* They ran in all directions, howling.

Bea came flying out of the night in her flannelette nightie, headlight ablaze, wide eyed, arms flapping.

"They brushed right past me on the throne," she said, indignant.

The visitors

WE'D COME TO THE place for the place itself, unaware of the bearing human contact would have on our lives, prepared to do without for months at a time.

Aside from the raucous interruptions from family and close friends over Thanksgiving, Christmas, and Easter, October to April was a simple duet of our own thoughts, debates, or silences, punctuated by sundry animal noises.

Even through the quiet of winter, though, people remained a presence. We had, aside from what we recalled from summer visitors, much to know them by, especially the letters and books they sent so we could curl up on the couch with a lady detective from Botswana, a circus elephant trainer, a *Confederacy of Dunces* (Louisiana Joe had sent us that one, saying he'd known the author), or a *Black Swan*.

The human feast was, in that way, year-round.

In winter, of course, there was time to ponder, to recognize contrast, and sometimes to decode what had not been obvious.

The two of us had come to the island to seek (the sea, open space, more of each other) more so than to hide. Some of the loners we had encountered had come here to hide, it seemed, the better to seek.

Our regular, for instance, the friend of a friend who ritualistically dropped by each year in his beautiful handmade baidarka yet kept pretty much to himself on Mel's beach. Or that other man we saw but once, tending to an elaborate, perfect camp and fire ring on that same spot at Mel's. Though he had very little to say, he mentioned the work he had time away from: he was an opera set builder. He was quiet, possibly sombre. Just before he left, he came across the peninsula to present us with all sorts of brilliant gear he said he'd no longer need.

Or the middle-aged man who, on several occasions, arrived by inflatable, alone with his young son, and set up a remarkable tent of his own design, a long tunnel equipped with a little wood stove. A thing to behold. But most impressive was his devotion to the child.

How different those three were from, say, Gerry's or Yves and Patti's joyous private groups with their giant cook-ups or exuberant surf play.

The bonded pairs, even those we knew well, gained fresh definition, as we had, from being here in the open, pistachios out of their shells.

Deakins brought Deanna, Chris brought Cec, Irene brought Albert, Graham brought Barb, and Godfrey brought Vivian, who, although she despised any sort of discomfort in the outdoors, paddled out with him anyway. Easter holiday, lovely conditions. Sure enough, the weather broke, hard, just in time for their return trip to Tofino. They had an epic such that Vivian publicly accused Godfrey of attempted murder. She didn't mean it, of course; and they have been bickering happily ever since.

There were couples here to celebrate. The young folk from Lantzville, for instance, who'd just completed the second half of a Vancouver Island circumnavigation; or the mature pair who seemed so intoxicated by love, so drunk on each other's voice and intellect that we felt like voyeurs at our own table. (Would these two ever, ever call each other a Luddite or a dickhead like the two of us?)

Vargas Blues: We had had a
spell of blue light one year, in
the thick of winter. But this blue
spell, heralded by a curious oval
halo glowing around the setting
sun, lasted a month in the early
summer, seamlessly reflected in
the seasonal lagoon.

Several kayak writers, old friends or new, had come by, some to stay.

With Tim and Tory, the encounter was random. They had set up camp by the river in cold, windy, wet weather. His plan had been to introduce his Ontarian wife to his passion, kayaking the west coast, a nostalgic journey for him. She was, however, newly pregnant, and too green with nausea to appreciate her new surroundings. We proposed the Appendix. Only after smoke had begun streaming from the chimney did we proceed with the proper introductions. Tim turned out to be the editor of a kayak magazine. The weather took a turn for the worse, they stayed on. It led to a friendship. In time, they sent us home preserves and a rock from Ontario's Bruce Trail to add to our shell path. A puzzle for some future wandering geologist.

As for Lee, the nostalgia ran way back. On his first visit to us with Margie, to mark his birthday, he called his mum from Fingers, right where he'd camped thirty years before with a pioneering group from Seattle. Lee was one of those engineers spat out by Boeing in the 1970s who'd turned their energies to kayak design and retail, then, in his case, to writings on navigation. Our friendship was longstanding. He had a gift for simple practicality, demonstrated this time by a handwashing station he set up near the outhouse. It went like this: ladle water from the pail into the opening at the top of the round hanging fish float, then rub your hands under the small hole at the bottom. Things he'd made, improvised windvanes and the like, dotted the coast wherever he'd camped.

Of all the nostalgia–time-travelling folk we had hosted or come upon on Vargas, though, none spelled the feeling more clearly than petite, bookish-looking Marianne, who had a lover named Dude. Dude was in fact a Shirley, a spectacularly handsome, chisel-faced, icy-eyed woman with a partly shaved head and this particularity that from a small wart on her cheek there emerged a neatly tied off braid of hair. A high school science teacher and a biker, she was celebrating a significant sobriety anniversary upon our first meeting. Marianne, who had kayaked the area before, was sharing favourite places with her. We took them in for tea and a meal, and saw them again on two or three subsequent years. And then it was Marianne alone, revisiting old memories, bringing her usual gift of olivetta. Her quiet mourning was heart-rending.

Also grieving a loss was Neil, our cross-island neighbour at the Vargas Island Inn; Marilyn had died suddenly.

In all the years, we had never walked the trail to their side; we had heard their news second-hand through groups that stayed with them. Operations there had wound right down now, although the couple next door, who'd been part-timers, had now retired to Vargas and could keep an eye on things.

top Black oystercatchers, sentries of the outer shore.

bottom Evidence of teredo worm.

OUR NEIGHBOURS ON THE FRINGE
THE INTERTIDAL

LIKE OUR YEAR-ROUND NEIGHBOURS the black oyster-catchers, we spent much time poking around the intertidal zone—rocks, tidepools, seaweed beds, and exposed sands— looking for things to eat, consider eating, or simply admire. It was all there, either on full display or hiding in crevices or under rocks, wherever we looked or trained a camera lens.

Tidepool Encounters

Behold, first, the orange sea cucumber, *Cucumaria miniata*. We took turns visiting it each day, waiting for that special moment when it would deploy its frilly tentacles for a feed of plankton. Its predators are sea stars.

Ochre and purple sea stars share their pools with green anemones, a surprising match given both are fierce carnivores. One anemone displayed its gut for the camera. Of note: the anemone's mouth hole doubles as its anus.

Further notes

The ochre and purple sea stars enjoy keystone predator status, lording it over the mussel beds.

They are capable of such tricks as jettisoning a limb and regrowing it within a year, and can in fact regenerate themselves from a single limb. Thus, they can live two decades, if seagulls and sea otters give them the chance.

Their well-clad neighbour and competitor, the Lewis moonsnail, dweller of sandy bottoms, drills tidy holes in mollusk prey to suck out their contents. Unfortunately, its rubbery, collar-shaped egg cases are sometimes mistaken for beach litter.

Beach Ephemera

Crossing the beaches between tides often revealed strandings, some tragic, some not.

opposite Clockwise from top, left: A handsome jellyfish; a jumbo mussel sporting two types of barnacle; a by-the-wind sailor; a squid's egg mass the ravens left unsampled; and Sponge Blob.

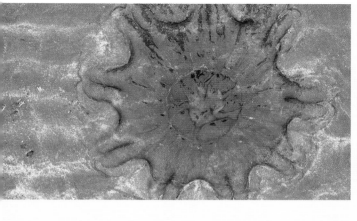

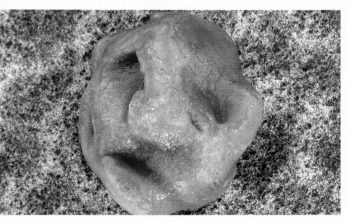

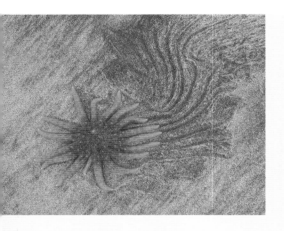

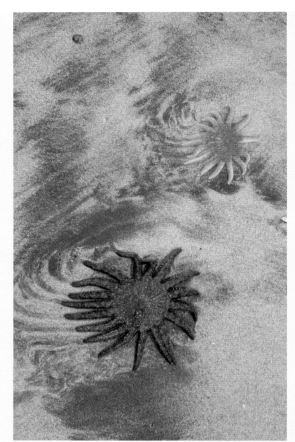

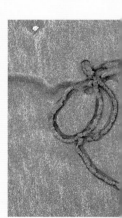

Works in progress

Mink and sea otters left paw prints across the sand, seals their belly drag marks with chopped margins. Colonies of tiny bugs did lacework, crabs worked at track making. So did sunflower sea stars, the star performers in that field.

The most dedicated worker on our beach, meanwhile, was the inch-long purple olive snail, *Olivella biplicata*. Between tides, the master engraver tunnelled around in search of meaty bits, its works ranging from tidy and small to massively complex, occupying the whole foreshore when the tide was lowest.

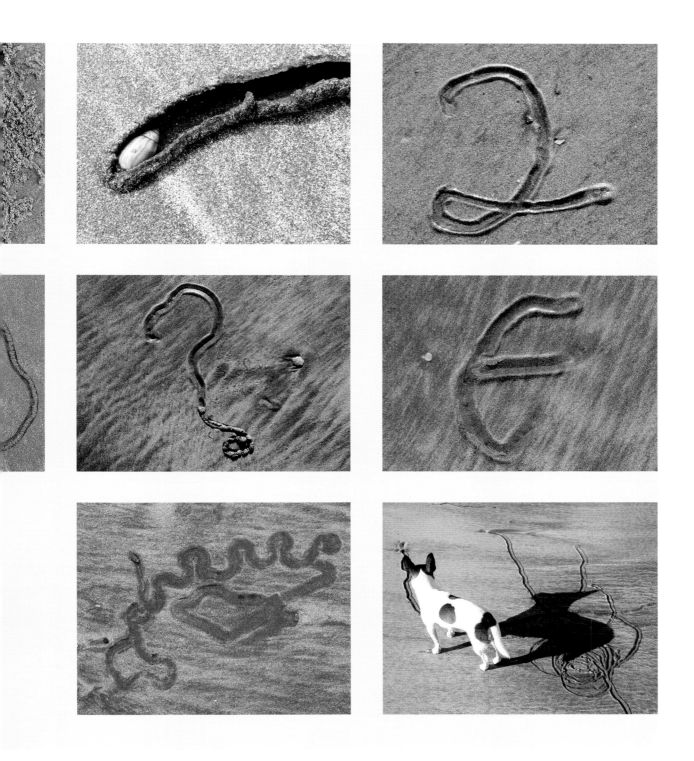

A misfit on Sometimes beach,
otherwise called a glacial erratic.

8

MOMENTOUS CHANGES

I WAS HELPING OUT at the Seattle Boat Show when I first met *Blackie*. She was beautiful, all black above the waterline except for a stainless steel motor guard, and I lusted after her from the moment we were introduced. She was 7.1 metres long with a powerful hydraulic motor on each of her three wheels and a button in the middle of her joystick that, when pressed, acted like a diff-lock on a four-by-four truck. She had a windlass at the peak of her bow and black rope looped along the top of her tubes.

The thought of moving on to a new boat had me fantasizing happily when, a few days later, I was being prepped for surgery at Nanaimo Regional Hospital.

Something had gone badly wrong in my hip one day when I was running on the beach. I limped home, and it didn't get better. I eventually consulted Dr. John, who referred me to a specialist.

"How long did you say it had been hurting?" the surgeon asked, looking at my X-ray.

"Maybe a year."

"I'm surprised you could walk at all. You're down to bone on bone. You're going to need a new hip."

And so one was installed.

Bea was left holding the fort for the next weeks. Olympia took the ferry across to Nanaimo and waddled into my hospital room with a bouquet. By then, she appeared to have a beach ball stuffed up her jumper, her baby due in two months. We made quite the pair.

Across the Pacific, a nightmare.

opposite Promise after the storm.

When I was released, Dawson, who lived in Nanaimo, drove me back to Tofino, where Greg took me in for a further week of recovery and physio torture.

Greg was a kayak friend from way back, a reformed adventurer now working for the Friends of Clayoquot Sound, where he had been the one to accept the "no logging" donation from the tugboat operator. In the 1980s, he had contributed two articles to our kayak quarterly, one on paddling the Northwest Passage, the other on circumnavigating the Hawaiian Islands. Later, in one of life's remarkable coincidences, Les the Aussie captain had run into him somewhere in the Red Sea and described him as "some crazy Canadian bloke in a home-built open dory, who carried an umbrella for shade." That dory trip, started in Canada, had ended in a shipwreck on the Moroccan coast.

Greg had since turned the page on such capers, spending his time writing, fighting for the environment, and eventually serving a term as a Tofino town councillor.

After my three weeks away, I walked our beach without a cane. I was still pretty stiff, though, and for a while it looked like one leg was two inches shorter than the other.

"Not a problem," Dr. John assured me, "they'll even out eventually."

SPRING EQUINOX, our grandson Leo emerged, and we went to Vancouver to greet him and check up on Olympia. The gathering of the clan included Drs. Pam and John, who "just happened to be in town," and could they come and check the baby? The new parents were managing well, so after a few days, we headed home to relieve house-sitters Yves and Michel, who had been speaking French to our animals.

Bea couldn't resist the grandson magnet for long and headed back to Vancouver three weeks later. It was my turn to stay home. It was raining hard, Tofino style, when I dropped her off at the bus terminal. Sheets of water lashed the sea and obscured the hills as I drove the little inflatable home. The tide was low when I arrived, and the beach flat and streaming water. I ran the surf and pulled ashore.

By the time I had the canoe cart in place at the bow, the stern wheels were down to the axles in liquefied sand. To get it moving, I had to lift the boat and motor so the wheels cleared the sand, then rush forward and start pulling before they sank again. This

MARCH 11, 2011. We have the radio set for 3:00 AM as usual and get news of a magnitude 9.0 earthquake off Japan's east coast. A tsunami watch, then an advisory, is in effect for Canada's west coast with waves possible by 7:00 AM. Low lying areas of Hawaii are flooded as waves crash ashore and several California marinas sustain heavy damage. We are spared, though the ocean swirls ominously for days afterwards. We check on our Japanese friends. None have been directly affected, though Take cancelled a surf class he had scheduled that day.

Sendai. Fukushima. The tidal wave. The thousands of deaths.

HOUSE NOTES—AN EXCERPT
Dogs, cat, and chickens

DOGS ARE FED on an as needed basis. Dog food is kept near their dish (they share). Replenish water bowl as required (by the door, under the bench). When wolves are around, we lock the dogs in at night. They have sleeping mats upstairs but will likely try to hang out with you in the guest cabin. Bungie gets cold around 4:30 AM and may try to get into bed with you.

Lolita has her own window seat in the house but is not allowed on the orange couch in the living room. (Bungie is.)

If Lolita is hanging out with beach campers (her summer job) she will need to be brought home in the evenings. (Otherwise she will bark at wolves all night.) Bungie tends to stay with her own people.

CAT is fed morning and evening—one handful each time. Food is in the brown bin on the porch. Her name is Vargas and she is charming but slightly autistic. She lives outside but will ask to come in if there is wind or rain. There is a litterbox inside (under the bench near the dog dish) but it gets so little use it won't require your attention.

CHICKENS: (Only two left.) We feed them each morning with grain (½ cup put inside the coop, in the metal bowl) or scraps (such as leftover salad, grass clippings, berries). Grain bin is by the door in the vestibule.

Aunty Beth, the smaller chook with the gammy leg, is as likely as not to die on your watch. Do not eat her. She can be sent off on the outgoing tide (tell her she will be remembered as a good hen). Please note: hens are now retired and will not provide you with eggs.

Make sure there is water inside the coop as Aunty Beth may not go out at all.

would gain a metre to a metre and a bit, by which time I was gasping for breath and all four wheels had sunk to their axles. Clearly this needed rethinking.

I dragged three sheets of plywood from the workshop and put one under the rear wheels and one under the front wheels with the third forming a plywood road. The boat moved easily for the length of a sheet so long as a wheel did not slip off. I would then move the rear sheet to the front and gain another two and a half metres. Part of the problem was that I could only pull using my good leg. The doctor's words kept coming back as I dragged the gammy limb sideways up the beach: "Remember now. You need to take it easy for the next six months."

At low tide, it's a long
way to push ... or pull.

It took three hours to pull the boat to the boathouse.

Meanwhile, Bea was treating herself to a private French film festival on Netflix and the choice of two possible flush toilets at Dylan and Sarah's posh condo, where she tended their cat while they were overseas. She spent the days with Olympia and Leo and doing shopping for items we needed. When she came back several weeks later, she had on a new pair of granny glasses and, in her wheely suitcase, supplies of tea and Macedonian feta, leather for new chair covers, and piping trim and felt backing for our otter skin project.

Walking the beach one morning, we'd found the body of a sea otter. It had a fatal propeller wound on its neck and we were lucky to reach it before the eagles. The fur was exquisitely soft and so dense you could force it apart with your fingers and not see skin.

Non-Indigenous people were not supposed to possess an otter pelt, but it seemed a greater crime to waste it, so I skinned it out and cured the pelt in the traditional way, using the brain of the animal. It would make a fine gift for Leo, given its water (and pee) repellant qualities.

It was Goode, our friend from the Primitives, who'd explained how to use the brain of the animal to cure the stretched, dried hide, a laborious process of soaking, drying, and breaking (softening). They say the brain of an animal always has enough grey matter to tan its hide. The process uses no salt or other chemicals, just grey matter mushed with water and rubbed into the hide.

Another treasure we had found was a remarkably straight five-metre yew log jammed among lesser logs midway along Mel's beach. It was more than twenty centimetres in diameter with rings too close to count, a deep red-brown, and so dense and heavy it was hard to imagine it floating. I could barely move one end and figured next time I had the chainsaw on that beach I'd cut it in three pieces and take them to the boat to transport to our beach. I pointed it out to Aron when he came with Olympia and Leo later in the spring, mentioning how perfect it would be for projects.

Next day, Aron turned up at the workshop, dripping sweat, with the entire log on his shoulder. He dumped it down proudly then proceeded to swim out to Burgess to cool off and look for eagle feathers under the nests. Clearly he could get more use out of my fancy free-diving gear than me, so I gave it to him.

There was much jubilation that summer, with visits from regulars and other good friends. Deakins was ecstatic: his book, *Making Sense of Us*, had finally appeared and he was thinking about the next one. Lee and Margie spent a week teasing the salmon. A New Zealand nephew visited with his family. But behind the happy chatter, the good-eating, and the clinking of glasses, there was a new sense of fragility. The horror of the Japanese tsunami had rocked us; the footage, watched and rewatched, of a community just across from us, devastated by a wall of water. The thought of the debris field floating toward us ate into us, though it would take another year to reach us. We made a concerted effort to clear new growth and blowdowns from the tsunami escape path at the north end of the beach.

The Beseeching Tree.

opposite Portrait of a dream.

The Pulling Together event, combining Indigenous and RCMP paddlers.

MARLIN CALLED one day to ask if we would take some pictures of an unlikely-sounding venture between Indigenous paddlers from around BC and the RCMP. They were expected on our beach next day, some paddling traditional-design canoes Marlin had built from fibreglass.

A colourful flotilla of more than twenty boats turned up, with up to ten paddlers in each. Some canoes were painted with designs typical of their home village and many of the paddlers wore traditional clothing. The surf was mercifully light and the weather easy on the weary crews that had just paddled from Tofino on their way to Ahousaht.

Lolita was so excited by the carnival atmosphere she had a seizure as she raced across the shallow lagoon.

"I think there is something wrong with your dog," an officer said.

Lolita lay on her side twitching, eyes rolled back.

"Oh, she does that occasionally," said Bea, "but she'll soon get over it."

Sure enough, after a few moments, a subdued Lolita stood up on wobbly legs and joined the party.

An expensive-looking RCMP cabin cruiser managed to get stuck on my favourite fishing rock as the operator attempted to drop someone ashore. The RCMP had a reputation for doing

New friends: a canoeing family.
ANDREW HOLOTA

clueless things like that in Tofino because the force liked to move people on as soon as they became comfortable in boats and chances were that their replacement would be from Saskatchewan or Manitoba. Fortunately, there were many willing hands to lift and push the boat off the rock, and the damage appeared light.

It was the tenth year the Pulling Together event had been held and this was the most ambitious to date. It involved over 250 participants journeying on the outside to Ucluelet and up the long canal to Port Alberni. Unfortunately, contrary winds and cold rain resulted in a tow from accompanying motorboats, and some catch up by road.

Around this time, a new wolf issue emerged; another black one, smaller than the pack leader. It began to hang around our beach, often parking itself in front of the house like a big dog waiting for supper. It was not getting the right sort of attention from Lolita and sat there so stupidly Bea named it Bozo. It appeared to be a she, either mistaken about Lolita's gender or else a clueless provocateur. She'd been a concern to campers at various beaches, so Francis took a special interest in her, and he turned up one day with a new deterrent, a paintball gun. Bea just had to have one.

Another black newcomer joined us in early August: *Blackie*, the very same boat I had drooled over in Seattle. I was, by then, the

A new arrival put to work.

opposite Changing winds
bring in the sea fog.

Canadian West Coast agent for the brand, something I could do from the beach thanks to smartphone technology. I found a business accountant in Port Alberni and traded in our small pickup for a beefier one, capable of towing a heavier boat and trailer. Bea was less than enthusiastic about the project, pointing out that if what we needed to achieve the simple life was an expensive boat, then maybe we shouldn't be on Vargas. I was having way too much fun to hear that message. Besides, some people pay more than that for a house.

Blackie could go places other boats couldn't. At sea, she was even better than the 6.1-metre model with a top speed of over 40 knots and enough length to manage big seas on the outside and larger surf on the beach. She could skid a twelve-metre alder for firewood like a tractor, and the all-wheel-drive feature dealt with soft sand and enabled her to climb over logs the size of power poles.

AFTER EIGHT years on Vargas, we were starting to consider taking some time off each winter and discussed the idea with three potential house-sitters. It never got beyond talk, but for the first time, the thought was there. Dylan had come to his own conclusions and taken to sending Bea real estate listings.

Our New Zealand niece, Debbie, and her daughter spent the start of September with us, then we all went to Vancouver together for a big event—Dylan and Sarah tying the knot. Friend Godfrey and two of his daughters would be house-sitting (no Vivian this time), and late morning, we passed them on the water. Soon after we hit the road, news came over the radio that a 6.4 had just struck fifty kilometres offshore. We called Godfrey.

"Earthquake? What earthquake?" he said.

In October, the completion of the Maaqtusiis subdivision across the way was celebrated with a traditional feast and ceremony. The project included, notably, the first asphalt-paved roads in Ahousaht. What we could see through binoculars beyond the thin fringe of trees was standard suburbia. There were lampposts emitting bluish light and even the occasional police lights flashing. In the past, the only evidence we had had of our neighbours had been the occasional slow beat of drums from Bartlett and a soft glow in the mist above Ahousaht some nights.

CLOUDS OVER CLAYOQUOT

NOT LONG BEFORE we moved to Vargas, Chief Earl Maquinna George published the book *Living on the Edge: Nuu-Chah-Nulth History from an Ahousaht Chief's Perspective*.

His chapter on traditional territories and the treaty process introduced the "Song of Tiskin, the Thunderbird." This was a song handed down to him over many generations, from Chief to child, and is now sung by Nuu-chah-nulth Tribal Council members before every meeting at the treaty table.

We had not heard the song on Vargas, but we had seen Tiskin hover above Flores and Catface in the form of a cloud. And sometimes a thick grey mantle, strangely layered, settled on the summit of Catface.

Although by spring of 2011 the Yuułuʔiłʔatḥ (Ucluelet) People and their four neighbours in the Maa-Nulth First Nations group had finalized their land claim settlement and treaty process, the Ahousaht First Nation, like most Indigenous Peoples in BC, were still at the negotiating table. In 2008, however, they had achieved a five-year interim agreement (the New Relationship), related mostly to forest development and resource revenue sharing. As of 2007, both logging tenures in the area were controlled by Indigenous companies, Iisaak Forest Resources Ltd. and MaMook Natural Resources. We often saw tugs pulling giant log barges past our beach at a ponderous pace, usually at dusk, once in conditions so rough we reached for the camera. During the preceding tenure, the Ahousaht First Nation had negotiated a land swap with the Weyerhaeuser Company for community expansion; the land at the north end of Marktosis Reserve was unsuitable for new housing because of the landfill occupying the middle space. Thus the Ahousaht First Nation's dwellings had returned to the open coast.

Agreements of other kinds were in place.

In the inlets, just recently, a fresh protocol agreement had been achieved with Cermaq Canada, the multinational operating more than a dozen fish farms in Ahousaht traditional territory. Its main purposes were employment on one side, operational stability on the other. Although the fish farms were mostly tethered in out-of-the-way spots, their huge ecological impact and distinct lack of tourist appeal prompted fierce debate. The elected Indigenous government was at odds with the Hereditary Chiefs; one championing development, the others stewardship.

The issue most troubling to us, our nightmare, was the open-pit copper mine proposal for Catface. Imperial Metals had gone ahead with six drill holes in 2010, shaking up sizable opposition. The plan was to lop off the summit and dump the tailings into the Sound.

"Think of it," a local booster was suggesting. "After extraction we could have our own Butchart Gardens right here in Clayoquot, a first-rate tourist magnet."

The question was, how keen were the Ahousaht people to have those jobs nearby?

left Thunderbird flies toward Catface.

middle The mantle cloud; beneath it, a proposed copper mine.

right Logging remains a feature of Clayoquot Sound.

I WAS returning from showing *Blackie* to a customer in Parksville. It was getting dark and the weather was atrocious. With the windshield wipers slapping full speed, I tore through the fading light on the twisty Tofino road hoping to get home before dark. Not a chance. I did not relish the prospect of having to spend the night in my truck with no sleeping bag. Staying in a hotel would have been the smart thing, but I never seriously considered it. Besides, I suffer from the "heading for the barn" affliction, a perverse form of stubbornness.

By the time I reached the boat launch, the night was dark as a mine. Rain thrashed the parking lot into agitated puddles by the glare of the headlights. Bea would not be expecting me, so I decided I'd give her a surprise. I pulled my dry suit on in the back of the truck, put on my PFD, and adjusted my headlamp. *Blackie*'s inboard motor came to life with a comforting roar. I backed off the trailer and drove down the ramp into the water, then started the outboard. Halogen lights built into the hull at the bow illuminated a billion raindrops like frosted glass. With luck, they would show a floating log in time to cut the motor, but not much else.

The GPS screen lit up and I adjusted the dim so I was not blinded by it. The little black dart on the screen was *Blackie* in the middle of the channel heading for Vargas with sand banks or rock on each side. I had a particularly powerful headlight, but as soon as I switched it on, the night became a blizzard of white as every raindrop reflected back at me. I switched it off and eased the throttle, bouncing my attention between the screen and the reach of the hull lights.

Rainwater streamed down my face. I sucked it from my moustache. At this speed, it would be a slow trip. The GPS showed my position off the rocks in Elbow Bank, then through the narrow gap between the button islands I'd been through a hundred times before. This time I couldn't see them. My faith was in the little black dart on the electronic chart.

When I rounded Eby I was shocked to see all was dark where the lights of the house should have been. Something was amiss. Large waves broke randomly around me. I swung north to avoid the bar . . . still no lights on shore. I'd been relying on them to get my line of approach. Now I was driven by a need to find out what was wrong.

There was a time lag on the GPS, so I waited in the lee of Burgess Islet for the satellites to confirm that I was not about to land on the south rocks. Then I started the inboard engine and gingerly approached where the GPS said there was a beach beyond the wall of blackness. A steepening wave lifted the stern. The bow dipped so the headlights lit the sea a vivid turquoise. Ahead, the wave broke, and I eased the throttle forward to stay on the back of it. At the same time, I lowered the wheels. With a thump, they locked in place. I gave the outboard full power. Behind me, a large wave broke, catching up fast. With all wheels down I could do eight knots. The bow wheel touched sand, then the rear ones. We were driving. I cut the outboard and raised it. As the boat left the water, lights came on at the cabin.

Figuring I would not be travelling, Bea, opting for an early night, had switched off the generator moments before I got to Eby. And then, seeing my lights, she went back and pulled the cord, and pulled it again and again. A short wait and it stumbled to life.

The lights of home.

Who woulda thunk it?

opposite Off to the boat show.

Next morning, she added six words to our *House Notes* under "Generator." It now read, "Needs choke to start: *unless it has just been running.*"

Marlin and Mary, after hearing this dark tale, presented us with a chunky ten-million-candlepower search lamp that could light up the beach from one end to the other—enough to compete with the Joneses across the way. It came with warnings: "Lens becomes very hot during operation. Do not shine directly into eyes."

Bea and I were finishing tapas one night when there came a knock at the door. Dogs barked. We looked at each other in disbelief. Who could be out there in a mid-winter storm? Two fellows, drenched, shivering, and hungry. One we recognized as Dave, the driver for Tofino Bus, a genial guy who'd chat with passengers all the way to the ferry in Nanaimo.

He and his buddy had gone to Hot Springs in a small inflatable. Locals favoured winter for their soaks there to avoid the crowds. Unfortunately, the iffy conditions for the run back to Tofino worsened as they hit the southeasterly in Calmus Passage. So here they were, company for the night, their boat safely ashore. Such is the power of a light on a dark sea.

One afternoon, months later, an aluminum runabout cruised past our beach from the south on another day that rare southeasterly blew over the island, chasing whitecaps down Calmus Passage and flattening the surf. We watched through binoculars as it vanished around Eby only to reappear a few moments later and, after some hesitation, run onto the beach in front of our house.

Someone brought an anchor ashore and a small group stepped out of the boat. The person with the anchor turned out to be Dylan, owner of Tofino Bus, a dedicated surfer and sometimes visitor to our surf break.

A very pregnant woman was among those aboard, at risk from pounding into the waves, so they needed a place to wait till conditions moderated. Conditions did not moderate that afternoon, so they spent the night in the Appendix, leaving their boat high and dry.

Next morning was calm, but their boat was two hundred metres from the water. Time to try something different, so we hooked up a towline, then dragged their hefty boat across the sand with *Blackie*. The long blue smudge left on the sand was from five coats of anti-fouling Dylan had just spent weeks applying.

Funny business

It had been the fiftieth International Vancouver Boat Show early that year but by the time I went to sign up, it was sold out. Next best thing was to take boat and trailer and position myself near the entrance to the main parking lot at BC Place. Each day, I would arrive at 6:00 AM and, for a twenty-dollar parking fee, I could not just show the boat, but drive it off and onto the trailer. It created plenty of buzz and lots of people took my card.

I then attended the Victoria Boat Show, which was indoors and more comfortable, but nearly cost us $13,000. Bea, whose smartphone was linked to mine, called me asking why I'd emailed our bank manager to have that amount transferred to an account in Georgia. Someone, it turns out, had broken into my correspondence files.

The Abbotsford Sportsmen's Show appeared better secured, fortunately, patrolled as it was with rod and gun folks in camo.

In all three places, there was lots of interest but, to my puzzlement, no sales. Not even when I participated in the Bowen Island parade, where the organizers loaded the boat with bikini clad beauties and *Blackie* led the procession.

Not even on Savary Island, where I came upon a local who had loaded his runabout onto a trailer, then bogged his truck down to the axles in soft sand. I hooked on and dragged his truck, trailer, and boat clear of the incoming tide.

Soon enough, though, I sold two boats to the owner of a beach property, and another to a buyer who wondered aloud that, forty years before, people laughed when they saw wheels on suitcases.

BC PARKS had suffered repeated budget cutbacks. Francis still did his regular servicing of campsites as he had since we moved to the island, but they had cut so much funding he no longer had two support crew. That was a safety issue. It took him two days to complete his rounds, rowing ashore alone while leaving the quarter-million-dollar boat anchored at risk from wind and current.

"Let me show you," I said.

We drove up onto the beach at all the sites he had to visit and had finished by 11:00 AM of day one.

"There's no chance Parks would go for this," he said sadly. "Even if it could pay for itself in a year, they wouldn't go for it."

Francis did offer us a gig as volunteer rangers on the Cleland Island Ecological Reserve, an eight-hectare rock with central tufts of vegetation and brutal exposure to the elements. Our task would be to help protect the distinct wildlife population, particularly the birdlife, which included two kinds of auklet, two kinds of storm-petrel, pelagic cormorants, common murre, black oystercatchers, tufted puffins, and pecky birds. BC Parks would pay our gas.

We were flattered by the offer and accepted the volunteer ranger baseball caps (who knows when they might be handy) and the Tim Hortons coupons compliments of BC Parks, but we passed on the enforcer role. We would happily remain Francis's eyes on the coast, however.

Doug Feathercraft, a former neighbour on Granville Island, offered me a task I *was* happy to carry out. It was to measure the

The perfect curl.

temperature of the sea, midway through an incoming tide every day, for a personal research project he had to cross-check official measurements of climate change. He provided an accurate thermometer and each week I would report the measurements. It became one of those comforting chores like feeding the chickens, and though I was unable to detect temperature changes, it was nice to be part of a larger effort that might provide some light for an overwhelmingly large project.

Exit the clouds.

9

PULLING AWAY

A DEBRIS FIELD OF 1.5 million tonnes, 3,200 kilometres long, 1,600 kilometres wide, had been coming our way. One year after the tsunami, a fifty-metre ghost ship was spotted two hundred kilometres off Haida Gwaii and the first confirmed Japanese debris item, a sixteen-year-old's soccer ball, landed on a remote island in Alaska. A month later, a motorcycle in a shipping container washed up on the northern shore of Haida Gwaii.

Beachcombing took on an increasingly uncomfortable edge as the flotsam began rolling in over the months. Each piece we came across held its own story of loss and sorrow, be it a fishing float or remnants of a building now populated with barnacles. The sense of humans being one family was searingly clear, almost physical. One person's tragedy is everyone's tragedy once the link has been made.[1]

There were lingering fears of nuclear contamination from the Fukushima plant meltdown. In addition, a specific warning had been issued to coastal populations: be alert to any and all hazardous industrial debris. There followed a list and an appeal to report such finds.

While we were on edge from such warnings, a weighty metre-long aluminum tube marked EXPLOSIVE! turned up. I took it (gingerly) to the boatshed, reasoning that if it could survive a surf landing on our beach it was stable enough to move. There was a Canadian phone number, so I called and spoke to the duty officer at Canadian Forces Base Esquimalt. They wanted the serial number of the device and, to my surprise, said I should not move

it and they would send someone out to get it immediately. That very afternoon, four black-hooded men in black dry suits arrived in a huge black inflatable with twin black outboards. Two of them swam ashore and sheathed the tube in bubble wrap before swimming it back to their boat.

"What is it?" I asked.

"Oh, it is just an old flare case."

"You rushed all the way out here from Victoria for a flare case?"

"Can't be too careful."

We still checked the campsites daily for less menacing items left behind, more often than not in the food caches.

On one occasion, Bea found a functioning floating VHF radio—and a bonus insulated mug of hot coffee—after a kayak party had set off through the surf. She successfully tracked down the owner.

When Mel turned up that year, he didn't seem the same. The catlike agility was gone, and his sister-in-law, whom we knew from several previous visits, was there to keep an eye on him and make sure he didn't climb ladders. A medical diagnosis would be dictating his next moves, she explained. The Vargas property was to be sold, though Mel was determined to fix the workshop roof first.

We had first option to buy, which we relinquished, with a certain sadness. Quickly, we set to work telling people we thought might be interested, folks younger than us.

Simon, a Vanier High Explore alumnus who'd made it big as a supermodel, had plans for an environmental field station on the island, but he picked a location on the protected side, leasing the old Inn initially, after Neil had died.[2] Dylan the businessman surfer was starry-eyed, and so was our Kate, but the timing wasn't quite right for them.

There was news in connection with Dick and Jane. Dick had died, and Jane had moved to the gentler side of Vancouver Island. Curiously, a son Dick had had from an earlier marriage had recently died here on Vargas, alone in a cabin on the other side, at Mud Bay. He had been watching television. We knew this from Dave the bus driver. Bus drivers know everything.

AT SOME POINT, Bea decided that enough was enough and stopped fishing.

Yielding to a greater force. (The root of the bullwhip kelp is known as a holdfast.)

One last cast.

"Too many salmon," she announced.

Our freezer was full, the kids' freezers were full, our friends all had frozen smoked salmon. I was, she said, becoming a beach feature, fishing obsessively.

As I saw it, my fishing rock both anchored and liberated me. Thoughts cycled through my mind, clarifying as I watched for surface clues—but she had a point about fish in freezers.

Bungie, meanwhile, had taken over as my fishing buddy. She would sit on the rock and watch the line. As soon as there was a salmon on, she would quiver with excitement and edge closer. Down would swoop Ibrahim and Fatima, who had been watching from the tree on the point. The three of them stood side by side, waiting for fish guts or gills to crunch up. Even in cold rain, Bungie would sit stoically on the rock, shivering, watching each cast, ears folded back. After two hours, she'd throw back her head and give a little howl. And we'd go home.

Bea had developed obsessions of her own. The first was photographing the messages squiggled in sand by dwarf olive snails feeding at low tide; her Vargas Island Purple Olive Snail Art Collective project. There was pleasure in this, but something more forlorn to her second obsession. In lieu of the usual beachcombing, she now looked for small rocks along the beach, selecting matching ones. This was her Family Reunification project. The rocks that went together stayed together in a baggie. She wasn't sure what to do with them after that.

The offering

A gift of light.

OLYMPIA HAD BEEN LATE attending to a ceremonial duty around Leo's birth, the Offering of the Placenta. Said placenta had awaited the right circumstances for more than a year in her deep freeze.

This trip, she had brought it along in a square plastic tub, popping it into our freezer overnight.

After sun-up, a group of us followed as she bobbed along the beach trail with Leo in a carrier-pack. We were headed to her place at Joe's.

On arrival, she built a small fire from her remaining cache of sticks and we had hot tea under the scraggly canopy.

Clambering over the rocks behind her campsite, we gathered by the rock pool where she had once tended a sea glass collection, bits of which were still visible, lodged in crevices, after the fury of four winters.

There were grassy patches between rocks, monkey flowers in wet spots, sun flashing over water, babbles from a baby. All was perfect.

Getting his feet wet.

above Birds of a feather.

right Sea and cloud, crepuscule.

There were quiet mumbles and short speeches of a celebratory nature, and then the placenta was released as a food offering to the creatures Olympia had once shared this place with. It went *plop* as it fell out of its container, a touch disturbing in shape and colour. Bungie waded in cautiously for a sniff.

Everyone laughed and we walked home happy, lingering in Mel's daisy slope on the way. By now it had trebled in size, and, standing in one spot looking upslope at all those flowers pointed the same way, one could get quite dizzy.

That summer, Leo discovered the garden and beach under his own power, barefoot and free, toddling happily from puddle to grass tuft, from huckleberry bush to henhouse. The dogs followed him everywhere, bowling him over on occasion as he zigged or zagged off to the next thing like a tiny drunk.

How different our perspectives, yet how similar our joy in the moment. To him, it was the wonder of discovery; to us, it was satisfaction at life unfolding as it should, at change begetting renewal.

THE TYPE of beach visitors had shifted over recent years, we'd noted. There were still the same school programs and courses, but fewer catered tours and fewer private groups. We missed Alex, one of Dan's students who for years had been our first solo paddler of the season, ambling up the beach with his distinctive rolling gait, like a bear out for a stroll. Where was *he* now?

"People are more into day trips," Marlin suggested. "Nobody has time to take ten days off to go kayaking anymore."

Surfing seemed to be enjoying a resurgence and stand-up paddleboards were in. We saw a few paddleboarders tempting fate on our side of the island; one was belly down on his custom board, paddling with his hands, baseball cap on backwards in full sun. Marlin had brought a pedal boat to our beach once, a craft which held potential as a fishing platform. Stand-up boards, not so much.

A new water taxi operator was offering deals on tourist dropoffs to the wild beaches of Vargas, so on two or three occasions large groups had come ashore on ours with oversized coolers and boom boxes. Labour Day weekend was uncharacteristically quiet, though, with but one couple turning up, dropped off by water taxi. A long way from the kayak carnivals of yore.

Though open to the wind, Dunes and Little Baja get a level of protection from offshore rocks.

Sea fog incursion.

One day, in dismal weather, we came across two people camped on Mel's lawn right next to his workshop. They said they were Ahousaht, a middle-aged man and his teenaged nephew, come from a city in the Interior. They had a small runabout and their camping gear looked fresh out of its box-store packaging. We expressed surprise at their choice of campsite, explaining the sticky spot it put us in as the property's caretakers, especially as their firewood choice was Mel's dressed lumber. The man took umbrage. "This is Ahousaht land," he said, and he was there to reclaim it. His nephew watched in silence.

We left them to their camping and gave Mel a call. He was sanguine. "Let me know if they haven't left by tomorrow," he said, in which case he'd call the Chief.

By morning, they had moved on, and we noted with some sadness that their fire had failed to catch properly.

It was surprising how few Ahousaht people we had encountered in all the years, aside from elbows rubbed in lineups at the Co-op or at Gary's Kitchen. Bea had chanced upon an Atleo working at the passport office in Vancouver; seeing his nametag she'd asked, and sure enough he was from a house on Matilda Inlet.

Francis, this year, had introduced us to Trevor, his liaison with Ahousaht First Nation, who would oversee repair and maintenance work on the Wild Coast Trail, among other endeavours.

The Ahousaht had projects on many burners; there was talk of a longhouse on Ahous Bay, and the community had negotiated ownership of the sixty-hectare Kakawis site on Meares, with plans for an ecotourism development.

Meanwhile, jurisdictional and environmental battles raged or sputtered on over fish farms, mining on Catface, and old-growth logging.

BECAUSE JOHN AND I were facing the prospect of a move away from Vargas, I became preoccupied with the concept of home. Where—what—was home for transplants like us, one from the Antipodes, one from back East? Were we wedded to BC? Did home even matter? Was home dependent on a house we owned, as we had the mountain cabin and no other place before or since?

John was loath to leave the beach house. "I'll move if we find something better," he had said, confident no such place existed. He was right, of course, and counting on the possibility that whoever bought the property would still need a caretaker. John would stay put, a barnacle.

"Somewhere nice is all we need to find," I countered. "Somewhere better for old people with metal joints." I thought, but did not say, *somewhere the Coast Guard wouldn't have to come to take our bodies out*. He and I both knew he would not want to perform caretaking duties on his own, so the possible next steps were mine to ponder. I'd have to drag him, claws out, into our future and was prepared to do just that. The kids were on my side. It was freedom and fish versus future and family.

In the fall, Olympia and I travelled to Quebec with Leo for his introduction to the Eastern clan; two weeks of visits to various folks in various places, some known to me, some not. There were elderly aunts and a godmother to check in with for what would likely be the last time.

Because of my house-and-home preoccupations, we booked two nights at a B&B in a small town I knew well from having crossed it often on the way to the family cabin on the lake. A left turn had been required at the precise intersection of our B&B: my mother's childhood home. She always intoned a special song, about the call of the mountains, when we took that turn.

An impressive red-brick Victorian with a wraparound verandah and a widow's watch, the house had witnessed great drama, and by the time my mother, the youngest in her family, had turned eighteen, it had been sold, from necessity. After being home to another family or two, it had served as an old folks' rest home until its latest incarnation. The B&B was now for sale. It was beautiful. It was an option.

I knew someone, an architect, who made a quilt to celebrate all the houses she had lived in. Did houses matter to me in the same way? A house is but a shell even when voices call from it, I decided. The space, the beauty around the house is what matters most. We'd have to look for acreage; acreage in BC, on Vancouver Island, because that was where home was, where we belonged.

A bird had come by,
looking for bugs.

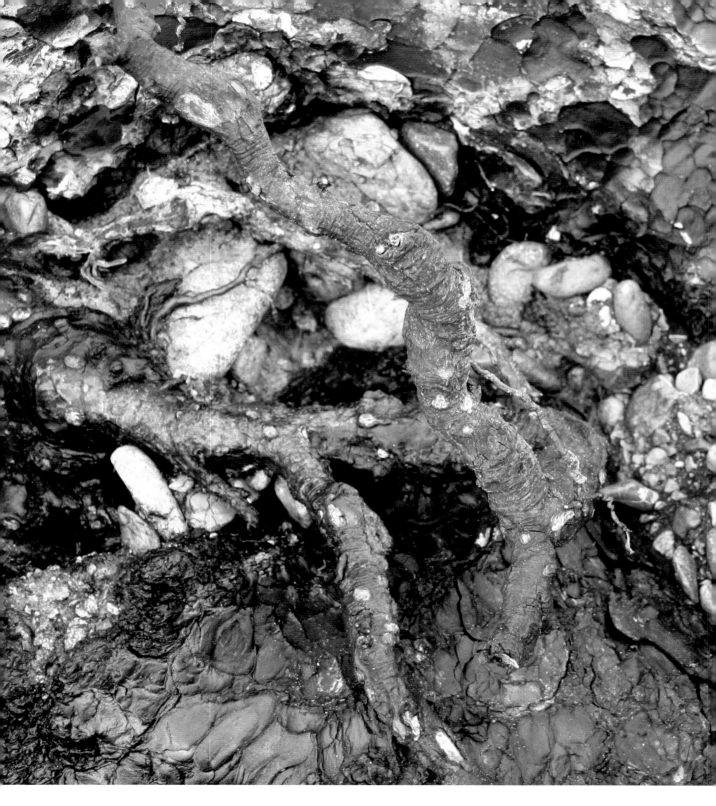

Uprooted tree: a study
on things held dear.

10

THE FALLEN CEDAR

BY FEBRUARY, WHEN I headed to the boat show, Dylan had found an acreage that might suit us south of Nanaimo. I stopped there on my way; two hectares with an old homestead. Was I ready for this? Bea would need to look at it after I got back. It was mostly up to her this time.

"Indoor plumbing," she said. "Worth looking at."

I'd booked space at the boat show in plenty of time this year. Instead of taking the boat on the ferry, however, I launched in Nanaimo and did the Strait of Georgia run to False Creek, pushed by a cold northerly. It took just over an hour. I drove straight out of the water and up the bank behind the Plaza of Nations. Dylan was there to film my arrival on his smartphone, and Aron, who also worked for the movies, put on his reflective vest and brazenly stopped the traffic on Pacific Boulevard with cones. I drove across the busy thoroughfare and up the ramp to the concourse, where I motored straight to my booth and parked.

I stayed in touch with Bea from the boat show, phoning morning and evening until, two days from my return, she failed to pick up. Concerned, I gave Dan and Bonny a call to see if they could check up on her. The weather was foul, so they called the Coast Guard to arrange for a wellness check, something we'd never had occasion to do.

Front desk with a view.

MY FLIP PHONE HAD flipped off for good, it looked like. I fiddled with it but nothing helped. I was not aware that taking the battery out and putting it back in might revive it. No worries; everything else was in order, I was cocooning happily in this dismal weather and John would be back soon with a phone that worked. In the meantime, I had the VHF for any emergency.

A day passed. I heard an engine and peered outside. The Coast Guard inflatable was at the southern rocks, dropping off two guys. I blanched. *Shit. Something bad's happened. Something's happened to John and they've come to fetch me.*

Sombrely, big umbrella aloft, I headed out to meet them. I could see it was Tom with someone I didn't know, approaching gingerly along the slippery rocks; Mat was out there practising surf manoeuvres. Tom had a first aid box with him.

"What's happened?" I asked.

They explained.

All being in order, we chatted for a bit. Then they went, and I was overwhelmed with a nauseating mixture of relief and embarrassment. Relief that no one was hurt, that help would come when asked for; embarrassment that assistance was felt necessary. This was a bit of a last straw for me.

I'd always dreaded the thought of the Coast Guard turning up, in part because of a story I'd heard second-hand about two officers' PTSD-level experience having to wrestle the lifeless body of a very large, naked woman down a steep and narrow set of steps. This was why I swore by my calf-length nightie: should I ever be found dead in my bed—as opposed to alert under an umbrella—I would travel down our steep steps properly shrouded in tartan flannelette.

WHEN I got back, Bea headed to Nanaimo, where Dylan and Dawson met her. The house was a go; too expensive, but we made an offer and it was accepted. Move in date, Easter weekend.

Someone was waiting in the wings to occupy the beach house after our departure: Jane of Dick and Jane's. She was terminally ill with cancer and Mel thought she might like to spend her last summer on Vargas. She saw it as a gift.

We began moving out gradually, delivering each boatload of goods to a storage unit in Tofino, ready for the eventual rental van trip to the future.

A cold embrace.

The Coast Guard hydrographic survey vessel *Vector* passes Monks Rock at a gentle speed. Home base: Sidney, BC. She entered service in 1967.

Ravens can live two dozen years. Would Ibrahim recognize the returnee?

I handed my water monitoring job to Dan. That spring, he and Bonny had founded their own environmental pressure group, Clayoquot Action. First order of business, No Tankers Tofino protests around the two big pipeline proposals in BC. That campaign had particular resonance with us. Our very first trip to Tofino as a family, some twenty-five years before, had been to help with beach cleanup after a major spill from a damaged tanker barge off Grays Harbor, Washington. Thick brown Bunker C sludge had fouled Vancouver Island beaches from Sooke to Nootka Sound. Locally, eight kilometres of beaches in Pacific Rim National Park required cleanup. Some of the tar balls and tar mats would have subsisted subterraneously on Vargas for years.

ON THE equinox, there was a great wind, and we heard a thundering noise behind the house. The Beseeching Tree had collapsed. We stood there for a long time, looking at where it had been.

Jane arrived a few days later, two loads of her goods brought in aboard *Blackie*. She was animated, quite radiant for someone so ill; a tall, substantial woman well wrapped in thick woollens.

Most of her possessions came in cedar chests. "Dick made those for me," she said with a shy sort of reverence.

There would need to be adjustments: for one, she had brought a box-store solar panel, ready to hook up to a sixteen volt battery system the house no longer possessed. We were in no great rush, so for a time we could leave her the generator—along with a dog and a cat for company if she wished. Chickens too. By then, we had replacement layers.

We asked the obvious question: why had she and Dick chosen to move away? It was done in great haste, under threat of death to them both, she said. Dick, although not without friends, had messed up on a few fronts and made serious enemies, one in particular who bore his surname.

The coast was now clear for Jane to return.

THE HOUSE we bought was built by Scottish homesteaders a decade before those at Port Gillam, well south of Nanaimo to avoid the devil's temptations in the rough mining town. There was a matriarch in charge, Mary. A photo given to us by the sellers showed her outside at her spinning wheel, two cougar skins hanging in the near background.

Tar and bad blood.

Copper beech leaves unfurling.

opposite New house, new dawn.

The sellers, a childless couple, were heartened we liked the house they had worked long and hard to restore yet some had dismissed as a teardown, impressed less than we were by its modern conveniences: running water, instant electricity, two indoor toilets, an indoor bathtub, and road access.

"We've seen ourselves as custodians more than owners," Judy had said with modest pride. Alas, with advancing years, the house had become much too much work for them. (They were, we'd noted, younger than us.)

HISTORIC WITHOUT BEING PRETENTIOUS about it, the house was a two-story wooden box on a stone foundation, kitchen tacked on to the rear. It was green like its surroundings.

Its only vanity was the front verandah, like the lace collar on the matriarch. From it, we saw riding horses in two separate fields, and between house and barn there was a large copper beech, its leaves unfurling their shine as we started moving in.

Aron had driven the big moving van across the island for us and helped with the heavy lifting. The floors here were clear Douglas fir, each plank the full length of the room. The glass in the sash windows was wavy, rippling like pond water. The ceilings were high.

The Turkish carpet needed professional cleaning before we could unroll it onto the parlour floor, so we took it in. Although it had had a beating each spring, it was full of sand. So amazingly full of sand, the cleaners said, that they had to send it off to the bigger machine in Courtenay. An hourglass of sorts for nine years at a beach house.

There seemed nothing nefarious about this house's history; it had gone from matriarch to adult siblings to a niece who cared for them in their old age, then became old there herself. After her death, the large acreage was parcelled off and the house rented out before our predecessors came along. There had been a hiccup during the rental period, when a dune buggy had been worked on in the parlour; the big window had been removed to let it through. A vague possibility existed that we'd find some scribble by the painter E.J. Hughes between layers of wallpaper; Mary had been his grandma and he spent childhood summers here. This was coal country, with slag piles visible here and there; but the mines were long gone, and time had worked to soften the tragic toll extracted by cave-ins, fires, and the bitter strikes of that era.[1]

Most surrounding parcels were two hectares (five acres), which in this place meant a mutually supportive community of neighbours with tools, helping hands, and advice to share. Strangely, one neighbour, Digger Dave, had grown up in Ahousaht and Quait Bay, where his family once ran a shake mill, then a lumber mill.

Our land was pleasingly diverse: fruit trees, lawn, and an organic garden; mature forest with Douglas fir, broadleaf maple, and Oregon grape; and, downslope, a patch of wetland choked with hardhack, red osier dogwood, and willow.

In the woodland, there were trilliums, yellow violet, bleeding heart, and vanilla leaf, with the odd little patch of fairy slipper. We'd have to find out where to look for chanterelles.

The main gardens were well landscaped, with large topiary specimens. Mel was impressed when he dropped by early on.

THERE WERE further trips needed to get all our things back from Vargas—two or three over the spring. Kayaks, furniture, and the garage tent needed retrieving. There were bags of recycling to dispose of and Lolita and Vargas to bring home. Jane did not need companion animals; a young traveller had moved into the Appendix to help out. Perhaps he had been sent.

In the end, there had been no chickens to reclaim. For reasons of her own, Jane had left the coop door open to the wolves. By then, however, we had fifty-five Rhode Island Reds at our end, rescues from a research program shutting its doors in Agassiz.

Aron and Sarah-bob volunteered to help me with one last trip in the small inflatable. Bea's list had included her boxes of family reunification rocks and assorted driftwood bits, which caused my helpers some mirth. "Looks like we're moving the beach," one said. On the way back, there was fog so thick we fetched up against a random island. I had to pull out my GPS to find where we were.

KAYAK FRIENDS OF OURS checked in on Jane over the months to see how she was managing and help where they could.

She was working on the house, we heard. Working, in particular, to get it back the way she remembered. The shell path, the wood-shed, the yew banister, the partition in the Appendix had gone, as had the rock garden bordering the house.

We were not offended. Or if we were, it was wrong of us. The house had her DNA, and she had every right to take this stand against the curses wrought upon her: change, Dick's death, her own so imminent. The circle was closing around her and she needed control, simplicity.

John still has moments when remembering Vargas Island hurts a little. Someone asked him once why he spent so long there.

"It gave me the impression of being free," he said.

Freedom matters, the sense of it, not the illusion.

House matters, the space around it matters—although their ownership more arguably ranks as a conceit. Like our predecessors, we are but custodians.

Being a pair, being here, protecting what we have matters.

As for home, well, it is what we make it.

Limpets: blending in, yet capable of locomotion

Winds of change.

POSTSCRIPT
A LAKE AND A RIVER

THE COUPLE ON Cow Bay suffered a cougar mauling six months after our move and left Flores after thirty years. Jane would have been on Vargas still, before her transition to hospice care.

Jane's helpmate stayed on for a bit, on and off, then a photographer friend of Dan's took on caretaking for a few seasons.

In October 2015, the *Leviathan II* was capsized by a large wave off our fishing spot near Plover Reef. Too large a group had stood on the top deck. Twenty-one people were rescued, six died. Two Ahousaht men fishing off Blunden Island were the first to respond.

There are sixplexes now in the Ahousaht subdivision; Wi-Fi as well. The Ahousaht First Nation now owns the resort at Quait Bay. Dan says Imperial Metals is keeping its Catface Mountain claim alive, waiting for copper prices to go up.

In time, Mel's property sold to someone from Denman Island, who set up a sharing arrangement with surfer Dylan, who himself had by then sold his Tofino buses. He and family now occupy our old house part-time. They have made many changes, some transformative. Audrey the cookstove was retired.

We have a wood cookstove here in Nanaimo; a brick fireplace as well. The old place is cozy.

We do not have a relationship with the territorial raven pair here, who share the local sky with turkey vultures. We relate more to a particular pileated woodpecker and the band of California quail patrolling our lawns and hedges.

In winter, our wetland becomes a lake; it is not the ocean but it mirrors light beautifully. Swans visit. In heavy rains, we hear the roar of the Nanaimo River, its waters home to steelhead, cutthroat trout, four species of salmon and, to the grandchildren's delight, crayfish.

Blackie found a new owner in Quebec and now plies the St. Lawrence where it widens out. Her current home base is the village where my paternal ancestor landed in the 1600s; a coincidence.

Dylan and Sarah-bob are a ferry ride away. They own two sailboats, a his and a hers. Olympia lives near us with her three sons. She is a widow now; Aron died at thirty-four in a work accident, alone in the woods.

Of the Vargas Island animals only Vargas remains. She likes being out here. She never cared much for the sound of surf. Young Missie, our new border collie, is doing her best to earn her trust.

In the room with the Turkish carpet are nine glass floats in a basket; on the wall hangs a watercolour depicting a certain tree.

The Nanaimo house, back and front views with snow.

opposite Ivy-leaved toad-flax, also known as wandering sailor. We'd found it among the boulders by Fourth Street dock, growing wild; and now, it is with us at the old green house, ready for new seasons.

The brass-coloured glass float
is from Shiretoko. The big one
washed ashore on Dunes beach,
and the littlest was the first.

ACKNOWLEDGEMENTS

WE OWE THANKS TO a great many people, beginning with Lucy Kenward for suggesting this story, Eileen Edmunds for helping us smooth its wrinkles, and Lara Kordic at Heritage House for speeding it to print with enough photographs to show the beauty our words failed to convey. For working their magic on the text, thanks to our editor, Andrea Lister, editorial coordinator Nandini Thaker, and our proofreader Marial Shea. Thanks to Setareh Ashrafologhalai, design wizard.

Thanks also to our children, with apologies, for their unwitting part in our retellings. Thanks and a fond salute to mum, Audrey, for her abiding interest in our doings and the pluck and smarts she applied to living. To the five Johns (four posthumously), for their sustaining friendship; and to Aron for the bright eyes, flashing smile, and boundless energy we remember him by.

Thanks to the Ahousaht People and all Vargas Island dwellers past and present for the wealth of stories. Our special debt of gratitude to Mel, and posthumously to Dick and Jane, for the house we called home.

Thanks to our house-sitters, hosts, and friends in Tofino and elsewhere: Glenn Mckinlay; Yves Aquin, Patti Stevens and Michel Guérard; Graham Shuley and Barb Gemma; Godfrey, Natalie and Bridget Forssman; Kate Hives; and our old friend Alain.

To Jean-François Marleau, Victor and Muriel Jones, Mike and Thea McGuire, John and Linette Smith, Deanna Dawson, Gerry and Diane Molnar, Paul Burke, Gary Bouwman and his neighbour Allan, Frank and Louise Quinby, and Irene and Albert Somody. To Joseph Guarnieri, and to Simon and Zoé in Quebec.

White sun, year of the guessing game.

opposite Gift from a wandering sailor, year of the three daughters.

To Marlin and Mary Bayes, Andy Holota, Noel Poole, Peter the pilot, Gilles Giusta, Tim and Kathy McGrady; to Martin Vseticka and Jennifer Moss, Wes Nicholls, Goode and Carole Jones; to Glenn Walsh of the garlic bulbs. To John Kimantas, Lee Moyer, Tim Shuff, and Tory Bowman. To Akio Shinya, Takehiro Shibata, and Takayuki Tsujii; to Craig Fraser, Paul Mitchell, David McKee-Wright, and Ken Schley; and to the sailor couple in Victoria who offered a bunk for a night. To dozens more for help with our projects or their contributions to our bookshelves, larder, or photo album. Among them, of course, the Explore group of Vanier High in Courtenay and the many Outward Bound folk who joyfully lent a hand.

In Tofino: to Dan Lewis and Bonny Glambeck, Cindy Cowie and Dave Weir, Greg Blanchette and the Shaw family, John O'Brien and Pam Frazee, Joanna Streetly and Marcel Theriault, Vince Payette, Tom Stere, Liam McNeil, Dylan Green, and posthumously to Dorothy Baert.

To Karedwyn and Paul Bird, Phil Mayes, Melanie McLeod, Catherine King, and posthumously to Wayne Adams. To Francis Bruhwiler for his common-sense approach, to Bob Hansen for explaining wolf behaviour, and to Maureen Fraser for offering day-old bread for our chickens. To bookseller Michael Mullen for sharing insights and taking delivery of our parcels, and to the Jacobsens for the cat Vargas.

To the many book authors whose material we have cited, paraphrased, and referenced in the text; in particular to Frank Harper, posthumously, and to Margaret Horsfield of Salal Books. To the photographers and friends who have contributed precious images; in particular, to bear and wolf whisperer Tim Irvin.

To Clayoquot Action, the Friends of Clayoquot Sound, and other environmental groups in the area, for their continued efforts and vigilance.

And to offshore people everywhere, for keeping their eye on the coast and their lamps lit on stormy nights.

Velella velella: on the dry.

L'AMI ALAIN

NOTES

Chapter 1

1   *Sea Kayaker* magazine was in print for thirty years (1984–2014).
    We co-founded it with Seattle partners, and jointly edited it 1984–
    1990. Ecomarine Ocean Kayak Centre closed its doors in 2019
    after thirty-nine years on Vancouver's Granville Island. We were its
    owner-managers 1980–1990.

2   July 2, 2000. At the time, within BC, the first documented wolf attack
    on a human in twenty years.

3   The poster *Wilderness—The Choice* helped raise funds for the Western
    Canada Wilderness Committee.

4   A Marine Very High Frequency (VHF) radio is a worldwide system of
    two-way radio marine communication and distress calls. A distress
    call on VHF radio will be heard by all other VHF radio users in the
    area as well as the Canadian Coast Guard.

Chapter 2

1   Chief Earl Maquinna George, *Living on the Edge: Nuu-Chah-Nulth
    History from an Ahousaht Chief's Perspective*. Ah-in-chut Shawn Atleo
    was the National Chief of the Assembly of First Nations 2009–
    2014. In 2008 he was appointed Chancellor of Vancouver Island
    University—the first person of Indigenous ancestry to be appointed
    as a university chancellor in BC.

2   Clayoquot Sound and its watershed extend from a bay near the
    Tofino/Ucluelet road junction to the Hesquiaht peninsula some
    fifty kilometres to the north. Three of Vancouver Island's fourteen
    Nuu-cha-nulth member Nations inhabit the Sound: Hesquiaht

First Nation, Ahousaht First Nation, and Tla-o-qui-aht First Nation (current populations 800, 2,300, and 1,200, respectively). The Nuu-cha-nulth population is thought to have numbered 30,000 in the late 1700s, at the time of first European contact. By the 1930s, it had plummeted to 2,000 as a result of introduced disease, warfare, and the dislocations brought about by the fur trade followed by a brutal colonizing process. The Nuu-cha-nulth Tribal Council currently reports a membership of 10,000.

3   For the record, Dylan disputes this characterization, saying it makes him sound exploitive and dickish. "The reality was much more nuanced," he says. "I loved Trim and had a fun time travelling with her on a leash, having her share a table with me and feeding her little bits of seafood from my plate. That this attracted female attention was an unexpected benefit."

4   The trusteeship for the National Outdoor Leadership School was a six-year commitment.

5   Ahousaht Hereditary Chief Shawn Atleo of the BC Assembly of First Nations led a fact-finding mission to Banda Aceh in support of Indigenous populations affected by the earthquake and tsunami.

Chapter 3

1   The first three videos can be viewed free of charge on YouTube, under "John Dowd sea kayak videos" or "John Dawson sea kayak videos." The fourth is stuck somewhere on Dawson's computer.

Chapter 4

1   M. Horsfield, *Voices from the Sound: Chronicles of Clayoquot Sound and Tofino 1899–1929*, 30.

2   M. Horsfield, *Cougar Annie's Garden*, 131.

Chapter 5

1   It turns out the McBarge (officially known as *Friendship 500*) was indeed used as a film location, serving as the lair of the Nightstalkers in the 2004 Marvel Superhero production *Blade: Trinity*.

The McBarge had spent most of its post-Expo life languishing in Burrard Inlet, visited by vandals and graffiti artists.

The historic tug *Ivanhoe*, built in Vancouver's False Creek in 1907, had a storied career working the BC coast. Like the McBarge she was featured at Expo, and at times at Vancouver's Maritime Museum.

In the late 1990s she spent a season as the kayaker mothership for a summer lodge in Nootka Sound. She was owned by Clayoquot Wilderness Resort from 2001 to 2014, dismantled thereafter. Her porthole windows are now reportedly in the lodge's guest toilets and her anchor on the front lawn.

Chapter 9

1   Worth noting: more than thirty BC municipalities have sister cities in Japan. We share much of the same fossil record.
2   The Cedar Coast Field Station.

Chapter 10

1   We now live on the ancestral lands of the Snuneymuxw First Nation, a Coast Salish People who have been here some millennia.

Quiet leisure.

BIBLIOGRAPHY

Abraham, Dorothy. *Lone Cone: A Journal of Life on the West Coast of Vancouver Island*. British Columbia: Dorothy Abraham, 1961.

Deakins, John. *Making Sense of Us: An Essay on Human Meaning*. Vancouver: Granville Island Pub, 2011.

Dowd, John. *Sea Kayaking, A Manual for Long-Distance Touring*. Vancouver: Greystone Books, updated revised 5th edition, 2004.

———. *Sea Kayaking: The Classic Manual for Touring from Day Trips to Major Expeditions*. Vancouver: Greystone Books, 2015.

Dowd, Olympia. *A Young Dancer's Apprenticeship: On Tour with the Moscow City Ballet*. Vancouver: Raincoast Books, 2002.

George, Chief Earl Maquinna. *Living on the Edge: Nuu-Chah-Nulth History from an Ahousaht Chief's Perspective*. Winlaw BC: Sono Nis Press, 2003.

Harper, Frank. *Journeys: Stories from Clayoquot Sound*. Tofino: Cherub Books, 2006.

Horsfield, Margaret. *Cougar Annie's Garden*. Nanaimo: Salal Books, 1999.

———. *Voices from the Sound—Chronicles of Clayoquot Sound and Tofino 1899-1929*. Nanaimo: Salal Books, 2008.

Kahn, Lloyd. *Builders of the Pacific Coast*. Bolinas & Berkeley Calif: Shelter Publications, 2008.

Lerner, Alan Jay and Frederick Loewe. "I Remember it Well" from *Gigi*. Warner Chappell Music, Inc., 1958.

Onley, Toni, as told to Gregory Strong. *Flying Colours: the Toni Onley Story*. Madeira Park BC: Harbour Publishing, 2002.

Pitt-Brooke, David. *Chasing Clayoquot: A Wilderness Almanac*. Vancouver: Raincoast Books, 2004.

Streetly, Joanna. *Paddling through Time: A Kayaking Journey through Clayoquot Sound*. Vancouver: Raincoast Books, 2000.

Close enough?

ABOUT
THE AUTHORS

New Zealand-born **JOHN DOWD** is an internationally renowned kayak expert, photographer, and the bestselling author of *Sea Kayaking: The Classic Manual for Touring, from Day Trips to Major Expeditions*, as well as several adventure books for youth.

BEA DOWD is a photographer and editor formerly involved in advertising, general publishing, and corporate communications.

THE TWO, a pair since the 1970s, jointly published and edited *Sea Kayaker* magazine, guiding it through its first half-decade in print. They also ventured into retail, selling sea kayaks on Vancouver's Granville Island.